CUSTOMER EXPERIENCE
STRATEGY
DESIGN & IMPLEMENTATION

By Maurice FitzGerald B.E.
With Peter FitzGerald D.Phil.

Copyright

Published in Switzerland
First edition, 2017

ISBN 978-2-9701172-3-0

Maurice FitzGerald Consulting
Chemin des Crêts-de-Champel
1206 Geneva
Switzerland
www.customerstrategy.net

About the authors

Maurice FitzGerald

Maurice retired from Hewlett Packard Enterprise where he was Vice-President of Customer Experience for Software up to early 2016. Before moving to HP Software in 2012, Maurice spent six years as a member of both the overall HP EMEA Leadership Team and the EMEA Enterprise Business Management Team. He implemented HP strategies that cross all businesses and functions, with a special focus improving Enterprise customer experience with HP. Other work included business strategy development for emerging markets, vertical industries, and a variety of transformational initiatives particularly in sales. He led the EDS / HP integration work for the Enterprise Business in Europe the Middle East and Africa. He has also worked for Compaq, Digital Equipment Corporation, and Blue Bell Apparel, the parent company of Wrangler jeans at the time.

Peter FitzGerald

After his Bachelor's degree in Psychology from the National University of Ireland, Peter went on to do his doctorate in Cognitive Psychology at Oxford University. Among the important things he learned was that he needed to paint with his left hand, rather than his right. He combined early work at the Max Planck Institute in Munich with the development of a successful career as an artist. He ultimately left psychology to work in the visual arts full-time, including thirteen years as the editor-in-chief of Ireland's leading art magazine, *Circa*. In addition to artwork, Peter also designs and implements websites and newsletters for galleries and other businesses. His website is at iCulture.website.

Acknowledgments

The last nine months spent writing this book and its two companion titles have been a fantastic learning experience. I learned how to transfer knowledge from my brain to my writing software. I also learned there is broad interest in my chosen subjects.

There are several people whom I must thank for their help and guidance.

First, of course, is my brother who did all the line drawings in all three books. His artistic ability and wry sense of humor come across well. Peter's years of professional experience as the editor of Ireland's leading art magazine, CIRCA, have also been invaluable. His eagle eye caught many mistakes I would never have seen, no matter how often I read the books out loud to myself.

Our test readers provided hundreds of improvement suggestions. I particularly want to thank Alyona Medelyan, Lindsay Hall, my sisters Una and Claire, Lena Palombo Forssell, Luc Vanden Plas, Matti Airas, François Gschwindemann, Michelle Tom, and David Jacques. Dale Halvorson, Dr. James Borderick and Ian Maddrell also provided much-needed encouragement and indeed stimulation to start writing in the first place.

And I can't forget my daughter Claire's great work on the cover illustrations. She, her sister Michelle and my wife Danielle have provided the support I need on the journey so far.

Contents

Foreword

It all started in a dark hotel room, as I struggled to sleep in the middle of a jetlagged night. I turned on a light, and looked at the note I had written myself earlier, telling me what city I was in. I had been working on software customer experience for a few years, and asked myself whether what I was doing made any sense. I was traveling to implement yet another measurement and feedback system, this time about individual software products. This came on top of existing competitive benchmark surveys, relationship surveys and transactional feedback. I asked myself whether I could name our top five improvement priorities, and found that I could not.

Creating and implementing business strategy had been my main work for many years. The essence of any strategy of any type, whether government, business, military or personal, is the concentration of your resources on a few things that really matter. Why had I not intuitively applied that approach to customer experience? Over the years, I had simply taken over existing teams, continuing and improving what they were doing. I never asked myself whether it was the best possible use of scarce resources. I never tried to articulate the top three improvement priorities across the entire business.

As I reached over to turn off the light, I saw the cover of the book I was reading: *Daniel Kahneman's Thinking, Fast and Slow*[1]. Kahneman was helping me to understand that all humans, including customers, do not behave as rationally as we might like to think. Reflecting, as I tried to get back to sleep, I realized that most companies, particularly in business-to-business environments, have similar problems. I dreamt of being able to combine strategy, customer experience and behavioral economics skills into a single methodology. That restless night was the starting point for this book.

---

[1] Daniel Kahneman: *Thinking, Fast and Slow*, published by Farrar, Straus and Giroux, 2011, ISBN 978-037427631

1. Introduction

1.1 What is this book about?

This book is about building and implementing a customer experience strategy in a business-to-business environment and in what I call 'the real world'. The real world is one where people behave like human beings, and not as traditional economists would have us believe. Human beings do not constantly try to optimize mid-term outcomes. They behave far less rationally, though still quite predictably. A great customer experience strategy combines scientific research, behavioral economics and the experience of others. In this book, I share mistakes I have made and things that I have found to be successful. Above all, I believe the book will save you a lot of time on your path to happier and more loyal customers.

What is customer experience?
In this context, customer experience is the overall impression your company creates with each of your clients. It is influenced by many factors, from the way your brand is perceived as socially and environmentally responsible, to what happens when someone complains about your product or service. From a practical perspective, it is about the 'customer journey'. It starts with the way a customer becomes aware of your existence and continues through the cycle of comparison, purchase, implementation, use of the product or service, decision to renew or repurchase, and their decision to talk about you positively, negatively or not at all.

Main concepts
The main concepts that will be covered are:

1. A comprehensive methodology for developing, communicating and implementing a formal customer experience strategy. The system works well for medium to large enterprises and can be simplified for smaller businesses. At least some of it is applicable to entities that have non-paying customers, such as government departments. Some

ideas on how to simplify the methodology for small companies are also covered.

2. A comparison of the main customer experience systems in use around the world, and a methodology for choosing between them. Each has been successful in its own way. There is no single correct answer that works for everyone.

3. A short chapter explores whether there is any evidence that employee happiness is a necessary condition for customer satisfaction. The research will surprise some readers.

4. Methods of ensuring you have the sponsorship required to succeed. Once you have a strategy, how can you be sure you will get and keep support for implementing it? What are the keys to keeping your management both interested and supportive of the ongoing investment?

5. Companies change constantly, from rebranding to mergers. How can they ensure customer loyalty through the inevitable transitions?

6. Since accurate customer feedback is critical to your efforts, there are chapters on the different types of customer research that can be used, how to design good surveys, and the most common mistakes people make when they implement their feedback systems.

7. The application of behavioral economics research to gain insights into customer behavior.

8. Examples of initiatives you may like to consider as you build your own strategy.

What is the scope of B2B?

For the purposes of this book, business-to-business refers to companies that sell products and services to other companies. Size does not matter much, though some techniques will probably not be appropriate for very small companies. My working assumption is that the client companies will be of all sizes, from small to very large. Strategy development will be faster for smaller companies with a small number of clients, though the methodology is independent of size.

What is this book about?

What is strategy?

Strategy is about how you deploy your resources to win. You don't have unlimited resources and can't afford to do everything. This book provides you with a system to determine what to do that will have the highest impact and how to implement it effectively.

✳A common but ineffective strategy is to "exceed customer expectations in all our interactions." Nobody has the resources needed to do this despite the thousands of web and printed pages that say the opposite. The question is how you determine where doing the strict minimum is appropriate, and how you will gain market share by doing something exceptional. It is absolutely not random.✳

Difference between customer experience and quality

Quality also tends to be defined broadly. People use the term for a wide range of different purposes. An excellent sales team could be said to be of high quality. For the purposes of this book, 'quality' means product and service reliability; their ability to continue to function.

This is not about organization design

Organization design needs to be done after work design. While I will cover possible answers to the question of where a customer experience leader should report, it is not a major focus of this book. I do, however, cover innovative ideas about staffing and how to make customer experience work into an attractive people-development path in your organization.

1.2 What makes B2B different?

"So what's the difference between B2C and B2B?"

"Sorry, that's not my department..."

This book is about customer experience in business-to-business (B2B) situations. Most of what you read elsewhere about customer experience is in the context of business-to-consumer, and is not directly relevant. The reasons are the following:

1. In B2B, a single person is never responsible for all the client organization's interactions with your company.
2. The difference in the relative financial importance of your largest and smallest customers is much greater than for B2C.
3. The people who use your products or services are usually not the ones who make the purchase decisions.
4. Your relationship with your customer requires more constant attention because multiple sales and support engagements are likely to be happening at the same time.
5. Relationships with individual people in the customer organization matter as much as relationships with positions on organization charts.
6. It takes time to know whether you are improving things.
7. Your customers want and need you to be successful.
8. Angry customers stay with you.

There are businesses that look like B2C but are actually B2B. Kentucky Fried Chicken (KFC) is an example, and so is General Motors. Most of their income comes from franchisees, not directly from consumers. Keeping franchise operators happy is more important to KFC than the views of the end customers. It is largely up to the franchise operators to keep the end customers happy.

No single person responsible for everything

When I shop at my local supermarket, I start by scanning my loyalty card and picking up my barcode scanner. I then scan each article as I put it into the caddy. I check out on my own, and speak to nobody. The same happens when I buy something from Amazon. More commonly, my retail interactions involve a single person. If I buy a pair of shoes, it is possible that I won't go back to that store for a year or two, no matter how happy I am with the shoes and the shopping experience. OK, if you want to be picky, a second person might have welcomed me to the store.

When a business buys from another business, things can be far more complex. Yes, a business can still buy Amazon Web Services and never interact with a human being. At the other extreme, a decision to no longer handle invoicing internally in a large company but to outsource it to another company can take two years. It can involve many different people, from the CFO to Procurement to labor unions at the customer end, from a sales person to an implementation project manager at the supplier end. And that is just to get to a decision. Implementation can be complex and involve a lot of different people. Management and organization changes can call the whole project into question and delay things significantly.

Differences in customer size matter

In most B2B situations, you have customers who matter more to you than others. There are two main reasons some may be special. The obvious one is revenue. A typical Pareto curve means that 20% of your customers may bring 80% of your revenue. The 20% need to be treated differently from the 80%. While you might like to think this is in the case in B2C, it has a different scale in B2B. There are very few B2C situations where a consumer is spending millions with one company. The second reason a customer may be special is that they are the pilot customer for a new product or service. You need them to be particularly happy with you, so they are willing to recommend the new product or service to others. (Of course, you should not expect a B2B customer to recommend your product to one of their competitors.) Exhibit 1.1 below illustrates a typical B2B customer profile.

Exhibit 1.1

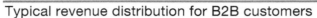

Typical revenue distribution for B2B customers

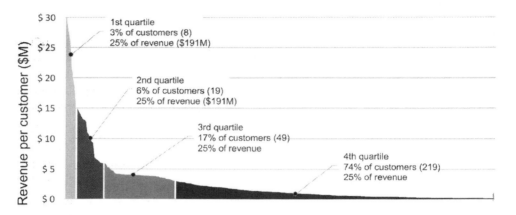

Users are not purchasers

Perhaps most importantly, the user of a product or service is rarely the one who signs the purchase order. If you are a catering company, you may bid to supply canteen / restaurant services to a large client. The people who eat the food are unlikely to be consulted in any way in the purchase decision. Unless your food is awful, they are also unlikely to be consulted at all about renewing the contract. Of course there are exceptions and end users can be decision-makers. A noteworthy example is software. Before the emergence of cloud computing, most decisions to purchase software required you to buy hardware. This meant that the central IT department could control everything. That has changed. An individual user can download a free trial version of some application and use it. It can spread to a department, if the department has a credit card, and then throughout a company, no matter what the CIO wants. That creates a specific customer experience dynamic which we will cover.

What makes B2B different?

Constant attention required ✳
The nature of large transactions and large projects means that some B2B customers require constant attention from your teams. The attention may be from different teams at different points in the implementation of a large project. Multiple sales, project and support engagements may be happening simultaneously. *auto system + Sceduling.*

Relationships with both positions and individuals matter
Large customer organizations are dynamic. Their structures can change, and people move from one position to another as they develop their careers. People you know at one customer can suddenly pop up at another. This has profound implications for research and improvement methods. For relationship surveys, it usually means that an overall score for a customer has no value. What matters is the state of each individual relationship, particularly with decision makers, decision influencers and to an extent with the end users of your product or service. The same applies in the other direction. Customers need to be carefully prepared for a change in 'their' account manager, for example. This will be covered in detail in the section on relationship surveys. If your customer project takes a long time to implement, you can be reasonably certain they will change their organization and that this will have an impact on what you have to deliver. Plan on it.

It takes time to know whether you are improving things
If you run a supermarket and want to improve sales of something, you move the product to the head of an aisle. You learn about your success or failure right away. When selling to businesses, it takes much more time to know whether customer experience improvements are helping or hurting. For most types of B2B businesses, it will take 12 to 18 months before you know whether a change is giving you a competitive advantage. The reason is the typical purchase cycle. Customers will use a product or service for some time before needing to buy more. If you are working in a company that considers thinking two fiscal quarters ahead to be long-term planning, you may have difficulty retaining the funding for your efforts. A later chapter covers methods for ensuring ongoing sponsorship for your work.

Introduction

Your success matters to your customers

Most of your customers want you to be successful. Think about the procurement people, for example. In their ideal world, they want as many companies as possible - including yours - to compete to offer products and services at the lowest possible price. Others want to see as many different innovations as possible, believing that your innovation will be to their competitive advantage. If you have already sold them something, your continued financial survival is important to their belief you will be able to support and improve your product or service. While the same may be the case in consumer businesses, consumers are more likely to have short-term relationships with companies, not caring much if one goes out of business. The consumer's livelihood is unlikely to depend on the survival of a company that does not employ them.

Angry customers may stay with you

Customer satisfaction is easy to understand in consumer businesses, less so when selling to companies. If the waiter in a restaurant treats you badly, most people (in the USA at least) still leave a tip and never go to the restaurant again. That is life in consumer land, apart from banks and cable TV companies that make it difficult for you to leave. Let's suppose your company supplies restaurant services to corporations. Six months into a contract, a customer's employee finds a worm in one of your salads. The customer gets angry. You devote large amounts of resources to fixing the issue so it never happens again. The customer stays with you. More about this in the next chapter.

1.3 How to stay married to your customers

It was Valentine's Day, and I was puzzled by the results of some HP customer experience research a few years ago. The data source and volume were impeccable. However, the results seemed to prove something that differed from everything that I had learned about customer improvement work. Putting the data and the date together let me learn something unexpected about how to keep your customers. While relevant to both, it applies more to business-to-business than business-to-consumer.

We were about a year into the implementation of the Net Promoter System under Meg Whitman's leadership as CEO of HP. The time had come to work out the relationship between our Net Promoter Scores®[2] relative to our competitors, and our revenue growth or decline (I will cover this exercise in some detail in the section on the Net Promoter System). We had eight years of benchmark NPS® data and could match it against corresponding revenue data for most businesses. We found that NPS was a great leading indicator of revenue. One HP business decided to investigate it in more detail. That business mainly had multi-year service contracts with its customers. The question they wanted to answer was "Which customers actually leave us?" They used their own relationship survey to understand the different behaviors of the NPS Promoters, Passives, and Detractors. What they found surprised us. I believe the findings apply to all businesses that have ongoing contractual relationships with customers.

From surprise to human relationships
Remember Valentine's Day had come around when I was dealing with the surprise. Here is how I rationalized it in terms of human relationships:

---

[2] Net Promoter, Net Promoter System, Net Promoter Score, NPS and the NPS-related emoticons are registered trademarks of Bain & Company, Inc., Fred Reichheld and Satmetrix Systems, Inc.

Introduction

The happy-happy couples

We all know couples who seem to be made for each other. I call them the happy-happy ones. They agree on everything. They have been together for years. We admire and envy them. In Net Promoter System terms, they are the Promoters. They are like the customers for whom everything is going  well. All major project milestones are being achieved early. The customers are getting more than the financial benefits they expected. They have been working with the same account team for years. Life is wonderful. The customers are references for us and bring us new business.

The couples who seem to fight a lot

Most of us also know couples who bicker constantly, needle each other, and occasionally provoke major arguments. In many cases, we are surprised to note that they have been together for years and show no signs of separating. Why? Because they are communicating! They stay together because they have invested a lot in the  relationship and changing seems too scary. In Net Promoter System terms. they are the Detractors. They escalate to the CEO. They get lots of attention. They get price rebates because they are angry. In the words of HP's former head of Global Account sales (Jan Zadak) "I love escalations! The customers always wind up buying more stuff."

When there are ongoing service relationships or investments in technology, the cost of change can be high. Imagine you have built all your business processes around the way SAP software works, but you now have a dispute with SAP. You will probably try to work it out. One of Meg Whitman's catchphrases as CEO of HP has been "Run to the fire. Fix it in 24 hours or escalate it in 48." I suppose it is also a guy thing that comes to the forefront in male-dominated industries. Men want to solve individual problems, and are willing to devote all their time to fixing a customer escalation, no matter what is happening in the overall relationship.

The couples in the deadly zone of mutual indifference

Have you ever been in one of these relationships? I have, in the distant past. You get home. You think to yourself, "She is not saying anything... everything must be fine." If you had that sort of relationship, how did it work out for you?  Communication is the lifeblood of couples and of B2B relationships. Think of it this way at the very least; if you are not communicating, your competition may well be. In the absence of communication, someone else smiles at your partner or customer and offers them flowers. They leave you, and you are surprised. Why did they not complain about something? What happened? In NPS terms, these are the Passives. Across most industries, they are 35 to 40 percent of all your customers.

What did the HP data show?

This multi-billion-dollar HP division had about a 15-point NPS decline over three years. Their revenue declined with the expected time lag. However, the surprise was where it declined. Revenue with Promoters rose slightly. Revenue with Detractors stayed flat. Revenue with Passives declined close to 20%. Someone else was smiling at our Passives and sending them flowers. For the sake of completeness, I should add that the particular business has since more than recovered the decline. I believe this data and these conclusions are representative of businesses that depend on renewable single-year or multi-year contracts. It is not helpful for pure product businesses.

The message

It is simple. Communication matters. Customers want to be remembered. If the only times your customers have contact with you are when you want to sell them something or when something is wrong, they will leave you. This could help your personal life too.

Introduction

Your customer experience listening and improvement system is a crucial part of maintaining ongoing communication with the customers who are not escalating, and who are not active references for you. Just as you would never consider delegating communicating with your partner to someone else, you should manage your listening and improvement process on your own. Don't delegate it to a third party. That would communicate something you don't want: "I am too busy to listen to you. Talk to this person instead. That is a good use of your time, but not of mine."

Win some, lose some

A symptom of the strength of your relationship is whether you win or lose new deals with existing customers. Understanding why you win and lose is the subject of a later chapter. We will also cover several ways of communicating with the customers in the 'deadly zone'.

2. Customer Experience Strategy

2.1 You need a strategy

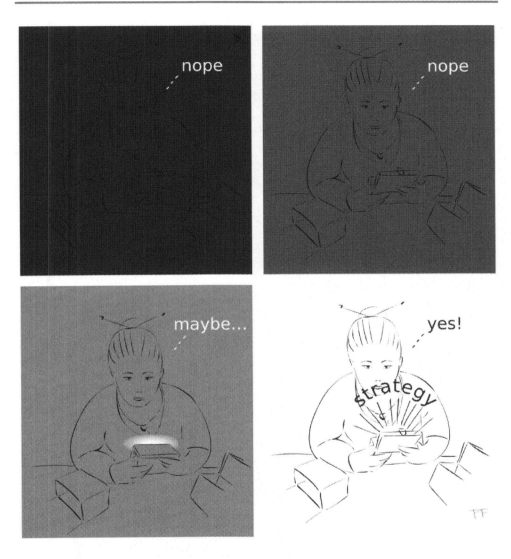

Customer experience strategy

Why bother with strategy?

The reason you need a strategy is simple: you do not have unlimited resources and never will. The word comes from the Greek strategos and means 'generalship'. Its origin is in how to deploy your scarce troops, equipment and diplomatic resources to win battles and wars. It is all about defeating the enemy. No general ever won a battle by saying, "I don't care where the enemy is, or what they are doing. I am going to line up my army three deep all across this open battlefield. I don't care what weapons my army has nor how they compare to those of the enemy. I don't care about the weather today or tomorrow. I don't care what my allies are doing. I have given my troops their top 20 priorities. We will just walk slowly forwards and I am sure we will win." Sounds ridiculous? It should. Unfortunately, this is what most companies' customer experience strategies look like.

Your enemies are outside your company

In business, your enemies are your competitors. The purpose of any customer experience strategy should be to do things differently or better than your competitors so you can win. The strategy should be articulated in terms of three to five priorities or initiatives that are easy to remember and make the biggest difference. The number of priorities is important. George A. Miller of Harvard published *The Magic Number is 7, plus or minus 2*[3] way back in 1955, suggesting that most people find it reasonably easy to remember about seven things. I find that teams in modern businesses cannot spontaneously remember more than five priorities. Think about this in terms of being able to list your priorities on the fingers of one hand.

Quick start

If you are just starting and don't have a strategy, here is how to go about generating one quickly. What follows is adapted from Willie Pietersen's book *Reinventing Strategy*[4] and his lectures that I attended at Columbia

---

[3] George A. Miller's article can be found at
http://www.psych.utoronto.ca/users/peterson/psy430s2001/Miller%20GA%20Magical%20Seven%20Psych%20Review%201955.pdf
[4] Willie Pietersen: Reinventing Strategy, Wiley, 2002, ISBN 0-471-06190-5

You need a strategy

Business School. I have used and improved the methodology for many years.

There are five steps and the following chapters cover them in detail:

1. Situation analysis: understand what is going on and what will change.
2. Make your strategic choices.
3. Secure the necessary sponsorship and investments.
4. Implement and experiment.
5. Start again.

What follows below are some things I have learned about the nature of strategy.

Resource limitations

As Pietersen explains, chess would not be an interesting game if you had unlimited resources. "Ah, you took my queen? Never mind, I have plenty more queens." The whole process is about using your resources as efficiently as you possibly can. Translating this to customer experience, statements like "We need to exceed customer expectations in every interaction they have with us" are both wasteful and unachievable. You don't have unlimited resources. You should not bother trying to exceed expectations on things that don't matter. Most customer touchpoints don't matter. It takes work to find out which ones do, and which ones can give you a competitive advantage. What matters for you will differ from what matters for your competitors. There are no universal answers.

The concept of hygiene factors

There are plenty of areas of customer interaction that are what I call 'hygiene factors'. The old explanation is to think about them like taking a shower. Nobody will thank you for taking a shower but everyone will notice if you don't do so for a long time. What this means is that there are things that just have to be 'good enough' but making them better will be a bad investment. Remedial phone support is an example. You need to be good enough at answering the phone and solving customer problems. Creating the capability to talk to them about past problems, or their birthdays and favorite sports teams does not add any relevant value. Similarly, delivering a product when a customer expects it is a hygiene factor. Delivering it early may be counterproductive and not worth the effort.

Just as standards of human cleanliness have changed over time, hygiene factors are evolving too. Yesterday's 'wow!' factor, like being on Twitter, may be today's basic requirement.

Never combine strategy and planning

A note of caution: never combine strategy and planning in a single exercise. 'Strategy and planning manager' is a common corporate job title. It has been my title in the past. When you combine strategy and planning into a single job, only planning gets done. When you start to do your strategy work just before the budget submission is due, your working team members will quickly start to say, "Forget this… just give me the spreadsheet to fill in." Strategy is a creative divergent process. By its nature, it is about doing things you are not currently doing. Planning is a convergent process. It takes what you want to do and creates order about doing it. Divergent and convergent thinking are diametrically opposed and should never be combined. Make sure you work on strategy at a time of year when planning deadlines are not creating pressures that will prevent you doing anything other than making minor adjustments to your current strategy.

Tactics can change, strategy should not

Once you have established a customer experience strategy, you must give it time to work. Just as marketing produces its results in the mid-term, the same is true of customer experience. This can be a challenging dynamic in businesses that are driven to produce results each quarter. Maintaining sponsorship for your work is both difficult and critical. Sponsorship is the subject of a section of this book. If you are creating a strategy where none exists, you will be under pressure to demonstrate results. The pressure is as much self-imposed as it is from other parts of your organization. The section on sponsorship includes advice on how to ensure your work continues in times of cost pressure, as well as times of growth.

You need a strategy

You know you have a strategy when the screaming starts
Deciding what you will not do is just as important as deciding what you will do. Ensuring you have the necessary resources will probably involve stopping existing work and transferring people and budgets to new work. It is inevitable that the people currently doing that work will be upset about the choices. Plan on this, and only be satisfied that your strategy is clear when the pushback actually starts to happen.

2.2   What you see is all there is

Before going into each step of the strategy development process, here is a special word about the data you use as a basis for your decisions. You must not assume that everything you have is everything you need to have.

The danger of WYSIATI

Nobel-winner Daniel Kahneman introduced the concept of What you see is all there is (WYSIATI) in his book *Thinking, Fast and Slow.* The concept is that we tend to make our decisions based on woefully incomplete evidence, believing that what we currently know is all there is to know. To use a Food Babe-type example (www.foodbabe.com), "The number of cancer diagnoses has multiplied by 20 in the last hundred years. Our diet has changed totally in that time. To cure cancer, we just need to change our diet." Just so you don't think I am picking on Food Babe (I am really), the following is equally illogical, "Life expectancy has increased by more than 20 years over the last hundred years. Our diet has changed totally in that time. Our diet is entirely responsible for the increase in longevity."

In the world of customer experience, the symptoms are easy to recognize, once you understand the concept. A senior executive who has never met a customer finally speaks to one. He / she returns to the office and behaves as though that one customer is representative of all customers. "The customer kept going on about the color of the timer buttons on our new microwave oven. It is really a serious issue. Send two people over to the customer right away to understand the issue better. This is our top priority. Cancel whatever your people are working on until this is resolved."

Another common WYSIATI statement you will come across is "Everyone knows that employee happiness is the most important factor in customer happiness." In a later chapter, you will see that employee happiness does not have much impact on customer satisfaction in most businesses.

What you see is all there is

I receive a lot of emails that include advice on various customer experience topics. A recent one was from Boomerang and provided *7 tips for getting more responses to your emails (with data)*[5]. While the tips are good, it would be a mistake to believe that these are the only seven things that matter. The study was limited in scope and did not cover things like personalization of the emails and the subject lines, for example.

Updating the elephant metaphor

You may have seen another way of representing WYSIATI. It uses the metaphor of a group of blindfolded people who try to identify what they are looking at by touching just one part of an elephant. The metaphor is helpful, but does not go as far as WYSIATI in terms of explaining the consequences of such limited beliefs. The drawing below uses more modern Virtual Reality technology and may help you to visualize how dramatic the effect can be. If you believe that what you see is all there is, you are not living in the real world, even when the zombie apocalypse is actually happening.

---

[5] http://blog.boomerangapp.com/2016/02/7-tips-for-getting-more-responses-to-your-emails-with-data/

3. Situation Analysis

3.1   Understanding your current situation

The first step in generating a strategy is a situation analysis. This is primarily focused on what is happening outside your company. For most companies, it should cover the six areas listed in Exhibit 3.1 below and lead to deep strategic insights. 'Insight' is a powerful word. Done correctly, you will understand the customer experience environment better and more quickly than your competitors, and make superior investment choices.

Set up the analysis
Ideally you will run the situation analysis in parallel in each of the six areas.
I suggest using small teams of people from different businesses or functions.
In a small company, a single person could do each one. The first meeting
should include all six people or teams and should agree on the questions to
be answered.

Exhibit 3.1

Situation analysis considerations

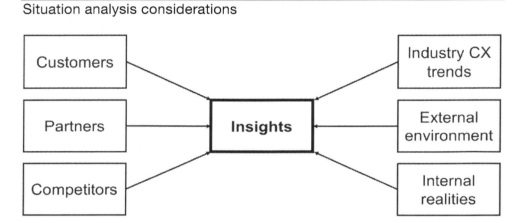

A potential agenda and methodology is suggested below. The most
important rule is that you can only get new answers by asking new
questions. If you ask and answer better questions than those your
competitors are asking, you will win. Hold progress reviews at least once a
week, in person or by phone. Experience suggests the first iterations will be
excessively superficial, with meaningless insights that your competitors
could easily achieve. You will know you have breakthrough when the
insights are few, powerful and the majority are things your competitors
would have difficulty implementing.

People who implement must do the planning
A fundamental rule of any successful project is that the people who will
have to implement the new strategy should also do the planning. This means
that the people who represent each relevant part of your company should do

so with the full authority, delegation and agreement of the person leading that entity. In addition to participating in the situation analysis meetings, your project management process should ensure that each person reports on progress to their own management every week. If you do not take this approach, critical stakeholders will reject the results of the analysis and you will be unable to implement. You should consider this carefully in the specific case where your business depends on resellers or implementation partners. You may like to invite some of them to participate in the exercise.

Let's consider each of the six areas in a little more detail. I have included just a few questions for each below. There is a more complete list in Appendix 1.

Customers

This team asks and answers questions about what customer experience expectations your customers have had up to now and how you expect them to change in the future. Here are some sample questions that may help get you started:

1. What experiences do your traditional end-customers want at the most important customer journey points? How reliable is your evidence for this?
2. How and why are the expectations of your traditional customers changing over time?
3. Are there useful ways you could segment customers and provide differentiated experiences to each segment? Should all customers of all sizes and from all industries be treated exactly the same or should you tailor a specific experience for each?
4. Should new customers be treated differently from existing customers? If so, how?
5. Do you have any information on how your traditional customers consider their experiences with you compared to what they experience with competitors?

At least half the day-to-day work of most customer experience teams is about listening to customers and partners, then summarizing what they want you to improve. This means that much of the necessary situation analysis information is directly expected from, and controlled by the customer experience leader. Naturally, in small companies, there is no single central reference point, except perhaps the owner or CEO.

Partners

The majority of companies have partners for at least some of their business. The three main categories of partners available to most businesses are resellers, implementation partners, and subcontractors. While you may have some partners who do not work with anyone else, it is more likely that you compete for their attention. Here are some possible questions that may help you to get started with the partner analysis:

- What are the critical touchpoints for your resellers, implementation partners and subcontractors? How have these been changing over time? Are these three categories useful, or is there a better way to segment your partners from a partner experience perspective?
- Should the top few partners, in terms of revenue generation, be treated differently from the rest?
- How do your partners' experiences with your company compare to that with your traditional and emerging competitors?

Competitors

There are two main categories of competitors: traditional and emerging. The emerging category includes companies you do not know about yet, but who may be about to take over your market. There are industries such as steel manufacturing where barriers to entry are high, and you are unlikely to be surprised. There are also low-barrier industries such as software, and pure import-export businesses. Here are some questions that may help analyze the competition:

- Do you have competitive benchmark survey data that lets you understand where your competitors provide a superior experience and the situations or touchpoints where you lead. If so, how do you compare with traditional competitors and are new competitors emerging with differentiated customer experience?

- How have competitors' customer experience strategy and results changed over time? What investments have they been making in people and systems? (Going to their website to look at their list of job openings may help with this.)
- What do your critical competitors say about customer focus and customer experience in their quarterly and annual reports? Is customer experience mentioned on their website as a formal part of their business strategy? How have they set up their customer experience teams and others that support critical touchpoints?

Customer experience industry trends

All industries change over time. Customer experience itself has been changing, from at least two perspectives. First, the products and service offerings that help companies to provide better customer and partner experience change over time. Second, there are industry-specific customer-experience changes. For example, 'Customer Success Teams' have been implemented by most large software vendors over the last five years or so. These teams help customers to install and understand software, free of charge. Here are some questions that should help this part of the analysis:

- What is happening in the customer experience industry? What ways of listening to customers are most popular? What new improvement processes and technologies are emerging?
- What is the impact of social media on customer perception of your products and services? Do you know what is being said about you on social media, and does it matter?

External environment

These questions are about the environment in which your company, your competitors and your customers live. It includes government regulation and general concerns and hopes of the people in countries where you operate. You may find these questions useful:

- How does government regulation affect the way you want to go about measuring and improving customer experience?

- What current and emerging rules about data privacy affect your current and potential survey processes?
- Do you know what surveys are being run in your company and whether they respect relevant laws?

Internal realities

While the first five areas are all about what is happening outside your company, you are unlikely to be able to sell and implement every conceivable idea within your company. These questions may help establish what you can achieve:

- What is the state of executive sponsorship for your current efforts?
- How likely are you to be to get any additional funding and people you may need to implement?
- What can you do to prove the value of your work?
- How can you secure enduring sponsorship for your work; sponsorship that will survive leadership changes?

Insights

The result of the situation analysis in each area should be a short list of insights. Each team should aim to have one to three insights and potential initiatives ready to explain and propose at the end of the analysis cycle. If a team has more than three 'top priorities', they have probably not put enough thought into it. As French philosopher René Descartes said when writing a letter to a friend (and this is often mis-attributed to Mark Twain), "Please excuse me for writing such a long letter. If I had had more time, I would have written a shorter one."

Useful insights often take the form of "so therefore…" statements. "We looked at the industry benchmark data from Temkin Group and saw that Acme is outperforming us in this area. We believe we are stronger than Acme here, so therefore here is what we need to do…" The point is that the action proposals need to be based on data and analysis, and not on ideas that have come from thin air, with no factual basis for believing they will improve customer or partner experience. Each team's insights and proposals will be competing with those from other teams for funding. The better supported the proposals are by fact, the easier they will be to explain.

Understanding your current situation

Addressing WYSIATI in situation analysis

WYSIATI has major implications for situation analysis. The quality of your insights depends on the completeness of the questions you ask. If you do not ask questions in a critical area, your strategy will be defective. A good question to add in each working session is ["What questions have we forgotten to ask?" Before looking at customer research results on a particular topic, you can reduce bias by asking what factors could matter for a decision. It will then be easier to spot things that may be missing from the research. It is even better to do this before you decide what to research. If you have a customer advisory board or simply a set of friendly customers, you may like to ask them the same question.

Situation analysis

A good technique to get your situation analysis in motion
Affinity Mapping is a simple and engaging technique for situation analysis. It is easy to understand and has the benefit of involving everyone in the room. While it can be used at the stage of each individual question, let's take the example of an initial meeting about the customer dimension of situation analysis.

The purpose of your first session is to work out what questions need to be answered. You absolutely need a facilitator to ensure success. The facilitator should direct the process, and should not provide any content. The equipment needed is simple: Post-It notes in two or three colors, a large whiteboard or large sheet of brown paper, and a flipchart, or another way of keeping the task definition visible.

Assume for a moment that you have explained the overall purpose and structure of situation analysis. The affinity mapping steps are as follows:

- Explain that the task is to determine what questions need to be asked and answered about customers.
- Each person to note a single question per Post-It, using full sentences.
- No limit to the number of Post-Its.
- Make them easy to read by writing in black pen or marker.
- Everyone to work individually, in silence, for five to ten minutes.
- When ready, put the Post-Its on the whiteboard.
- When all Post-Its are up, the team stands before the whiteboard and reads them.
- One person volunteers to group similar Post-Its together and explain the groupings. Others may move Post-Its or add new groups as needed.
- Team agrees the wording of the question that corresponds to each grouping.
- If you find a single question to be important and to have been treated too superficially, repeat the whole exercise to achieve better granularity.

- If you have separate teams for each area of situation analysis, they can work in different parts of a large room simultaneously. If you do this, the teams should explain the questions to each other to avoid duplication. At the end of the exercise, each of these teams should present to the others to ensure you achieve a single set of outcomes.

One tip I would like to add is that it becomes obvious if you have people who are not participating in the exercise. You can ask such people to lead the grouping exercise, for example. Try affinity mapping. You will like it.

Ensure insights are clear

Once the analysis of the six areas is clear, the top few insights and action proposals need to be documented for each. At this stage, the documentation can be simple. Define the work that would be needed to put the insight into practice. Estimate how many people and how much funding would be needed to do so. Make a reasonable guess at the potential timing. Reaching clear simple conclusions about a small number of priorities in each of the six areas will give you the 'long list', the total number of things that you could and should be doing to improve customer experience. We are now going to go into detail about the best methods of getting accurate information about what customers and partners want. That will be followed by simple suggestions on how to get from the long list to a short list of proposals.

4. Measurement and
improvement systems

4.1 Main measurement and improvement systems

The customer experience team should be your company's reference point for most customer research, whether for its own use or for use by the company as a whole. It is therefore critically important that the information used for the customer and reseller parts of any situation analysis be trustworthy. There are quite a number of customer experience measurement and improvement systems in use around the world. They are not all equal. This chapter covers some of the most common ones. Some consulting companies offer proprietary systems, and I cover their main measurement principle. There are wide variations in approach for these proprietary systems, but all have one common feature. The systems covered are:

- Smiley buttons
- Customer Satisfaction
- Customer Effort Score
- Net Promoter System
- Wallet Allocation Rule
- Consultant-provided proprietary systems
- Journey Mapping

4.2   Smiley Buttons

Smiley buttons are gaining popularity in consumer businesses and have only marginal potential in B2B situations. HappyOrNot and Agoraopinion are examples of companies who provide low-tech solutions in this area. Changi airport in Singapore has a more high-tech version. The general principle is that you tap on one of three or four emoticons to show how happy you were with an experience you just had. The first time I ran across it was in Heathrow airport, just after the immigration counters. They also have them just after security as you leave. If you are just looking for a number to track, this seems like a simple way. The challenge with the low-tech approach is that you have no idea why people are pushing a particular button so cannot use the input to drive improvements. Exhibit 4.1 shows a typical layout.

Exhibit 4.1

Smiley buttons

Please rate our service today

The weirdest place I have seen such buttons was at the passport control desks in Beijing airport. Theoretically, you are supposed to push a button while the immigration officer is looking at your passport. Really? Can he/she see you push the red button and what are the consequences?

Smiley buttons

In my local Media Markt

The HappyOrNot buttons have been installed in my local Media Markt electrical goods and media store in Geneva. They have been positioned just behind the checkout desk, facing the cashier. "Please rate our service today," The first time the buttons were there, my wife and I had had difficulty being served when buying an electric kettle. Were the buttons there for us to rate the service in the whole store, or just the check-out, which was efficient. The lady at the checkout desk did not know what was being done with the feedback. Once again, there was no way of indicating what we were happy or unhappy about, so no conceivable action could be taken by Media Markt.

Extracting value without providing any

I was in our Cambridge UK office one day when a US visitor arrived. She was only too pleased to tell me she had seen the smiley buttons just after immigration at Heathrow. I asked her whether there was any indication anywhere of the number of people who pushed each button, what they had learned, or what they were doing with the feedback. The buttons have been there more than two years now. As in all other situations where I have seen the smiley buttons, there was no feedback loop. They seem to be extracting value by having you push buttons, but are not providing any value back. There are plenty of people and companies who are not actually serious about improvements and just want a number. This seems like an excellent way to do just that.

Lest the above be perceived as excessively negative, note that HappyOrNot list some major companies as clients, including McDonalds, Microsoft, Lego, eBay and American Express. The references on their site[6] indicate some happy customers.

Emerging high-tech solution

When I last went through Singapore's Changi airport, I came across a somewhat better smiley system in the rest rooms and elsewhere. A touchscreen asks you to "Please rate our toilet" and gives five choices. If

---

[6] https://www.happy-or-not.com/en/

you choose Poor or Very Poor, you are taken to a second screen asking why and giving a choice among eight reasons, including the smell or lack of toilet paper. My Swiss half was worried about touching a touch screen that may just have been touched by someone who had not washed their hands, though the screen was marked "This screen is sanitized regularly." There did not seem to be any way to explain positive feedback, and there was no explanation about improvements that had been made from past feedback. A similar system using screens and software from Dr. Voxx is in Brisbane airport.

Relevance to B2B

There are very few B2B situations where you could ask your customer to push a physical button. The system could be used by government administrators that require you to go to their service counters to register your company or for other simple transactions. While you could clearly use smileys as your scoring interface for a web-based survey, this crosses the line into more conventional measurement systems. There is no real difference between asking a customer on your website to give you a score on a rating scale or on a smiley scale.

Conclusion

I can see the low-tech method as useful in a single situation, and this is A/B testing, where you are interested in finding out which of two things a customer prefers, and don't care why. For situations that require deeper insights, the low-tech system provides no way of finding out why customers provide specific feedback, and therefore has no conceivable use as an improvement system. If you only want to measure a score, but use other data sources to act on that score, it may fit your needs. The high-tech screens are an improvement and show promise.

4.3 Customer Satisfaction (CSAT)

When you are asked to rate your 'overall satisfaction' with something, you have entered the Customer Satisfaction rating system. The most common way of doing this is to ask you to rate satisfaction on a scale from 1 to 5, where 5 means 'extremely satisfied'. There is a minor challenge in the rating scale, as with all scales that do not contain a zero. A small proportion of the respondents will believe that 1 is the best rating, rather than 5. After all, you want to be number one, don't you? At the level of your overall brand, the satisfaction metric does not predict revenue as well as the 'willingness to recommend' metric used in the Net Promoter System. In addition, for surveys about telephone, web and chat support, the Customer Effort Score (see below) is a better revenue predictor.

"Top box" satisfaction

A common method of communicating results is to talk in terms of 'top box' satisfaction or "top-three box", for example. This means arbitrarily deciding that people who give you the top score, or the top two or three scores on a five-point scale are 'satisfied'. I have not been able to find studies of differences in customer behavior between the different categories or groupings. However, based on Net Promoter System studies, it seems unrealistic that someone who gives you a 3 is actually satisfied. The NPS research would suggest that someone who gives you a 5 is likely to recommend your product or service, and someone who gives you a four does not care much either way. A three would already be a sign of negative views. Note that some companies use seven-point scales.

The principal communication challenge

The lack of a single standard customer satisfaction scale and definition causes communication issues. It is quite easy to find companies that say "92% of our customers are satisfied." What does that mean? On a five-point scale, which of the five are they counting to get to 92%. Since there is no single definition, anyone explaining the metric has to explain where it

43

comes from, and risk losing time in an argument with someone in the audience who measures it a different way.

Composite satisfaction metrics

Predicting customer loyalty, meaning the desire of customers to keep on buying from you, can take different forms. The more sophisticated satisfaction surveys also include several questions that are not about satisfaction. The most common questions ask customer to use the same type of rating scale to answer questions such as "This company has earned my loyalty", "How likely are you to repurchase?", "This company is a leader in its field", "How likely are you to recommend this company or product to a colleague?" and so on. Several metrics can then be aggregated to form a satisfaction index. Where this is done well and with representative customer samples, it can be an excellent revenue predictor. We will cover some composite metrics in the section on proprietary measurement systems.

Lists of things to rate

Satisfaction surveys usually ask you to rate a list of things. The list can be very long. I participate in a survey panel that covers the travel industry. I have received surveys that only have satisfaction rating scales and took more than half an hour to complete. The main problems with lists of things to rate are:

- It is your list, not the customers' list. Most commonly, these lists are set up by the way your organization is structured. You want to get some sort of feedback for everyone. This may not correspond to what the customer wants to tell you about. Notably, if a competitor does something that you do not, only asking about what you currently do will prevent the customer giving you that feedback.
- It creates the illusion that each of the factors you ask about is equally important. It is particularly difficult to undo this subliminal message. Imagine you have 50 things that you ask customers to rate. Imagine further that seven of them have the worst rating possible. Once these 'red' items are visible, you will be forced to turn them around, even if they have no importance whatsoever.

4.4 Customer Effort Score

"Funny thing. While I was on hold it seems to have become more of a hardware problem..."

The Customer Effort Score is the metric described in the excellent book *The Effortless Experience*[7] by Dixon, Toman and Delisi. The primary focus is service-center work and the associated metrics. The authors present a compelling argument that what matters most for some customer interactions is how hard it is for the customers to get what they want. The single topic that surprised me the most was their data that shows that the majority of people who phone a company to get something done are simultaneously trying to resolve their issue or answer their question on the company website. Furthermore, you have to get to the 60+ age group for the proportion of simultaneous interactions to drop below half.

Delighting does not work ⚹
A central message from the authors is that "delighting" customers is pointless in most situations. Remember the main focus is customer service interactions. Their data suggests that delighting customers does not usually

---

[7] Matthew Dixon, Nick Toman and Rick Delisii: The Effortless Experience, Portfolio, ISBN1591845815

make them more loyal than <u>simply meeting their expectations</u>. They show that a service interaction is four times more likely to cause disloyalty than loyalty. You should take from this that the best service interaction is no interaction at all. As you build your strategy, think of another point the authors make, which is that/spending resources on <u>delighting</u> customers displaces those <u>resources</u> from things that are more important.

auto mation services

Best practices of low-effort companies

Particularly in customer service interactions, customers want to spend as little time as possible to get what they need. They just want to get on with their lives. The authors found four 'best practices' that were common to companies that successfully reduced customer effort:

1. Low-effort companies make self-service channels as effective as possible, minimizing the need to call in the first place. Personally, I dread phoning service centers, passing through ambiguous recordings that ask me to classify my request according to how their company is organized, rather than the problem I have, and spending long periods on hold. I do all I can to avoid it.
2. When customers do call, low-effort companies train their people to head off the next problem as well, based on their experience of what problems are likely to be related to each other.
3. These companies work hard on the delivering an appropriate emotional and psychological experience on the phone. In my reading, this is more about empathy than being nice to people.
4. Low-effort companies favor quality-related metrics for their representatives over volume and call-duration metrics.

Self-service

The key points made relate to the fact that most customers are happy to self-serve. Your company needs to work on how to keep customers in the self-service channel. Don't fall into the trap of just making it hard to talk to a live individual. When reading this, I was reminded of a story one of my INSEAD lecturers told us. He was asked to help Galeries Lafayette improve their customer complaint and suggestion system at their flagship store in Paris.

Customer Effort Score

At the time, Nordstrom was still relatively new and had made a name for itself with its process. My lecturer mainly seemed to copy the Nordstrom process, installing stands around the store where people could fill out a form with their comments. A management change happened after the project ended. The new management noticed the rise in complaints. Their response was to remove the stands and install a complaints desk in the basement. Complaints dropped dramatically. Success? Definitely not! The Effortless Experience authors suggest that the main improvement you can make to self-service is to simplify it, using several suggested techniques.

Conflicting metrics

I loved the book's message on the conflict between company metrics and human perception. Companies typically report first-contact resolution rates of 70 to 80 percent, while their customers report rates of half that. Some of this is because a different channel is used for the first contact than the one being measured. A lot of it is because the customer's real problem, say with an invoice being late, has not actually been resolved. Customers call back on related issues that they consider to be the same thing, but company metrics start from scratch. I have had this situation with Air France where in resolving one issue, they accidentally changed my street address in their system, so I phoned them again, using the same incident reference number. We fixed the address. They then closed the service event without resolving the first issue. I phoned again and had to start from scratch as they had closed the first event. The authors suggest a way of changing the metric definition, so that a repeat call is one from the same person within seven days, no matter what the reason. This seems like an excellent idea.

Training service reps

Training of the service center people matters a lot and quite a bit of what the authors describe works against classical metrics associated with reducing call time and getting as many calls done as possible per day. I particularly liked their work on personality-based resolution processes. (The customer's personality, not the service representative's.) Overall, I believe the book is essential reading for all service center leaders. It is experience-based and outstanding.

Back to the Customer Effort Score (CES)

The authors refer to their current metric as v2.0. It has evolved, both in terms of the question asked and the scale used. They tried many variations of the question and settled on one that translates well into most languages. With their current question, customer behavior changes radically by response. As they put it, "For instance, 94 percent of customers who had low-effort experiences reported that they would repurchase from the company, while only 4 percent of customers experiencing high-effort interactions reported an intent to repurchase." The Customer Effort Score is the response to the question, "To what extent do you agree or disagree with the following statement, 'The company made it easy for me to handle my issue.'" It is measured on a scale from 1 to 7.

Better than CSAT

The authors found that when comparing CES to Customer Satisfaction scores, across thousands of customers, CES was 12 percent more predictive of customer loyalty, as measured by stated intent to repurchase. They did not determine whether the customers actually repurchased.

Suggestion

If you are already using Customer Satisfaction as a metric in a service center, I suggest adding CES and tracking both for a time. Then compare trends with your financial trends to find out which is a better predictor of success.

4.5 Net Promoter System®

Fred Reichheld wrote his landmark article *The One Number You Need to Grow*[8] and published it in the Harvard Business Review in December 2003. He had spent two years investigating customer loyalty research. What he found was surprising and counterintuitive, at least at the time. Answers to a single question predicted customer loyalty and therefore revenue trends in most industries. A further finding was that "Our research indicates that satisfaction lacks a consistently demonstrable connection to actual customer behavior and growth." He pointed out that the American Consumer Satisfaction Index for Kmart, for example, continued to improve as it slid into bankruptcy.

Fred and his team studied 4,000 customers across 14 industries, using the 20 questions on the *Loyalty Acid Test*[9] questionnaire he had designed with his Bain colleagues. The study was about the actual behavior of people; whether they actually bought more and whether they actually recommended a product or service to someone they knew. In 11 of the 14 industries, a single question had the greatest statistical correlation: "How likely are you to recommend X to a colleague or friend?" In two of the remaining three industries, the recommendation question was just behind the top question. This surprised Fred, who had expected asking customers to what extent they agreed that "This company has earned my loyalty" to be the top-performing question.

Rating scale and behaviors

Even in the HBR paper mentioned earlier, Fred was able to do at least two further things. The first was to design a rating scale that was unambiguous. The second was to observe and categorize the behaviors of people who gave

---

[8] The One Number You Need to Grow HRB article can be found here:
https://hbr.org/2003/12/the-one-number-you-need-to-grow
[9] The customer version of the Loyalty Acid Test can be found here:
http://www.loyaltyrules.com/loyaltyrules/acid_test_customer.html

different ratings on his zero-to-ten scale. He found that people who give a 9 or 10 tended to buy more and to actively promote the product, service or brand. Those who gave a 7 or 8 were "passively satisfied" and tended not to say much. The remainder tended to speak and behave negatively, and he called this group Detractors. The Net Promoter Score became the percentage of Promoters, less the percentage of Detractors. Fred initially expressed this 'Net Promoter Score' as a percentage, and later dropped the percentage sign.

Partnership with Satmetrix

Fred worked with Satmetrix who began tracking 10 to 15 thousand recommendation responses from about 400 different companies in early 2001. In the airline industry, for example, the Net Promoter Score correlated directly and unambiguously with growth from 2000 to 2002. There were industries without such a correlation, mainly effective monopolies, such as cable television companies.

Evolution to a system

The HBR article evolved into the Net Promoter System, a Service Mark owned by Fred Reichheld, Bain and Satmetrix. Satmetrix also provides software and training courses that lead to certification as an NPS professional. The entire system was initially described in *The Ultimate Question*[10], now in version 2.0 and co-authored by Fred and Rob Markey, also of Bain. There have been a number of evolutions since the latest book was published and these have been described in some episodes of the excellent Net Promoter System Podcast. You can find the podcasts and many other resources at www.netpromtersystem.com.

Current state of NPS

Reichheld and Markey have made extensive updates to the system that have not yet been documented in a book. The first and most important addition is a second open text question. The result is a standard survey format for most purposes that looks like Exhibit 4.2. For surveys about an interaction

---

[10] Fred Reichheld with Rob Markey: The Ultimate Question 2.0, Harvard Business Review Press, 2011, ISBN 978-1-4221-7335-0

that has just taken place, Reichheld and Markey have added a rating question, "To what extent has your latest interaction changed your willingness to recommend?" just after the first recommendation question.

Exhibit 4.2

Standard NPS questions

- Dear Mr. Doe,
- My name is John Smith and I am the CEO of Acme. My management team and I want to improve Acme and believe you have valuable suggestions for us. Could you please answer the three questions below? When you click "Submit", you will get a summary of all responses we have received to date, and the top suggestions other customers have made.

1. How likely are you to recommend Acme to a professional colleague?

	0	1	2	3	4	5	6	7	8	9	10	
Very unlikely	◎	◎	◎	◎	◎	◎	◎	◎	◎	◎	◎	Very likely

2. Why?

3. What should we improve?

Main features

Other than the metric, the main features of the system as described in the book and in practice are:

- It is by far the most common customer experience measurement system. About two-thirds of medium to large companies use it.
- When implemented properly, there are only a few questions, so response rates are higher than in other systems with more questions.
- The Inner and Outer Loops for improving things for your customers and internally are well described and easy to follow.
- There are a number of sources of double-blind competitive benchmarks, making it reasonably easy to understand how you compare to others in your industry. Bain has recently started a process of certifying benchmark research providers. JD Power was the first to be certified for their methodology. Others will follow.

Measurement and improvement systems

Because it is easy to communicate, it is relatively easy to implement the basic measurement and reporting systems.

- If you need automation, there are loads of vendors who can help.
- The credibility of the system depends on your ability to establish the relationship between metric trends and market share trends. This is difficult to do, particularly if you have no measurement history. People have to trust you until there is enough data. That can take a couple of years, and you could lose sponsorship by then. Of course this would be the same with any other measurement system that claims to predict revenue.
- The main challenge is the analysis of the verbatim responses. Text analysis software should be used for initial screening and categorization to avoid human bias.
- Finally, because the system is simple, it is also quite easy to manipulate.

Personal opinions

I have worked extensively on the implementation of the Net Promoter System at HP. If I had to pick a single thing as its most positive aspect, I would pick communication. It is far easier to communicate how the scoring and system works than with any other system I know. My second observation is that who you ask matters. If you do not ask the correct people, the results will not predict your revenue correctly.

4.6 Wallet Allocation Rule

Authors Keiningham, Aksoy, Williams and Buoye describe the system in the book[11] of the same name. Its focus is a composite metric that combines the list of brands that a customer thinks of and their relative satisfaction with the same brands. Their research on the metric is sound and predicts share of wallet well in consumer businesses. While they focused on consumers, it seems reasonable to believe the same logic would apply to B2B situations. Even though the book documents some incorrect assumptions about how the Net Promoter System works, the conclusions are still valid. I consider this as one of several composite metrics that should indeed have better predictive value than NPS. All share the same issue of being relatively difficult to communicate, in part because they are not as simple or popular as NPS.

Six-step measurement and improvement process
Here are the six steps in the Wallet Allocation Rule process:

1. Survey your customers to find out how they rank you and the competitors they also purchase from. The ranking is based on their satisfaction, NPS or a similar metric. Since this ranking is the numerator, it is fair to say that the overall equation represents a sophisticated manipulation and improvement of the satisfaction or NPS score. Note in passing that the authors disagree strongly with what I have just written, but I believe no other logical conclusion is possible.
2. Apply the Wallet Allocation Rule to establish the share of wallet for each competitor.
3. Determine how many of your customers use each competitor.
4. Calculate the revenue that goes from your customers to each of your competitors.

---

[11] Timothy Keiningham, Lerzan Askoy, Luke Williams: *The Wallet Allocation Rule*, Wiley, 2015, ISBN 978-1-119-03731-6

5. Identify the primary reasons your customers use your competitors.
6. Prioritize improvement opportunities.

Let's consider these steps in more detail, comparing them to other methods.

Survey your customers to find out how they rank you

While the authors did this initially as a one-off high-volume exercise, it is hard to get this step to work well if you do the surveys yourself. If the survey goes out in your name as the authors suggest, the respondents will be biased in their responses. That bias will only affect the answers about your own company. There is no reason to believe the bias would affect the other competitors' scores relative to each other. You could of course use double-blind benchmark surveys administered by a third party. This is identical to the benchmarks survey method used for other improvement processes.

Apply the Wallet Allocation Rule

First, what precisely is the Wallet Allocation Rule? Exhibit 4.3 shows how it is defined in the book:

Exhibit 4.3

Wallet Allocation Rule calculation

$$Share\ of\ wallet = \left(1 - \frac{rank}{number\ of\ brands + 1}\right) \times \left(\frac{2}{number\ of\ brands}\right)$$

where

$Rank$ = the relative position that a customer assigns to a brand in comparison to other brands also used by the customer in the category

$Number\ of\ brands$ = the total number of brands used in the category by the customer

This should work as a predictive metric providing the customer continues to split their purchases among the same brands. There are industries that are relatively stable and where that logic is sound. There are industries with low barriers to entry, such as SaaS software, where it does not work at all. In fast-changing industries, you are better off using the relative NPS rank in the market, rather than by customer. IBM, Computer Associates and HP learned this the hard way. For many years, the three companies shared the majority of the market for system-management software. Then one fine day, Service Now came on the scene with a new type of software that required no new hardware to run it. They went from nothing to a market-leading position in just a few years, despite awful customer satisfaction at the start. Indeed, with the satisfaction ranking numbers they had in their first couple of years, the Wallet Allocation Rule would have predicted their quick demise. The Net Promoter System, with its focus on trend, correctly predicted the opposite. The source for this is double-blind benchmark studies carried out for HP by IPSOS.

Determine how many of your customers use each competitor and the revenue share for each

This exercise is useful in any case, if you want to understand what you have to gain and lose financially. One challenge is making sure your sample is representative of your customers as a whole. Are very large customers adequately represented? Do the people who responded to the survey actually have decision power?

Identify reasons customers use competitors and prioritize improvement opportunities

The processes described in the book for this have the merit of using a reasonably strong financial basis for justification calculations. There is a lot to be learned from reading the explanations. The belief that you will get the predicted financial result is based on a debatable premise, which is that competitors will do nothing while you are driving improvements. If competitors improve at the same pace as you do, you don't gain share, but at least you don't lose share. These issues are common to all improvement systems.

Conclusion

I don't believe the Wallet Allocation Rule method to be fundamentally different to the Net Promoter System. I like the fact that it relies on competitive rankings, and these should be part of a good relationship survey process in the Net Promoter System too. The calculations make the Wallet Allocation Rule more difficult to explain. The book makes questionable references and assumptions about NPS. The most fundamental issue is that

55

it states repeatedly that NPS does not use relative rankings, whereas *The Ultimate Question 2.0* repeatedly states that future market trends are predicted by NPS trends relative to those of your competitors. The difference between the two methods is that NPS takes a supplier-side view and the Wallet Allocation Method takes a customer-share-of-wallet view. They should produce similar predictions in stable markets. In software and other dynamic markets, I believe NPS will produce better predictions because it counts competitors that customers may not currently be using.

4.7 Proprietary systems

Various consulting companies propose proprietary measurement systems. The Temkin Group, for example, has both the Temkin Loyalty Index and the Temkin Experience Rating. They are useful examples as they both have one thing in common with the systems proposed by other consulting companies: they are composite metrics, aggregating customer responses to multiple questions. Since they are good examples, here are the details of what Temkin proposes.

Temkin Loyalty Index
From the Temkin website[12], "The Index is based on evaluating consumers' likelihood to do five things: repurchase from the company, recommend the company to others, forgive the company if it makes a mistake, trust the company, and try the company's new offerings."

Temkin Experience Rating
Again, from the Temkin website, "The Temkin Experience Ratings are based on evaluating three elements of experience:

- Success: How well do experiences meet customers' needs?
- Effort: How easy is it for customers to do what they want to do?
- Emotion: How do customers feel about the experiences?"

The Temkin Experience Rating report is available free each year on the Temkin site. An Excel file with all the data costs $395. Within the report, they state "To improve customer experience, companies need to master four competencies: Purposeful Leadership, Compelling Brand Values, Employee Engagement, and Customer Connectedness." It should be obvious and it is indeed stated that customers would never come up with such a list. The improvement suggestions come from a completely different

---

[12] The list of currently-available Temkin Group research can be found at http://temkingroup.com/research/

study. The Temkin Experience ratings are calculated using an average of the answers to three rating questions. Customers are not asked what should be improved. There is no claim that you can predict revenue from the experience ratings, though there is such a claim for their Loyalty Index. Exhibit 4.4 shows the questions asked, copied from the Temkin site with permission:

Exhibit 4.4

Temkin Experience Rating components

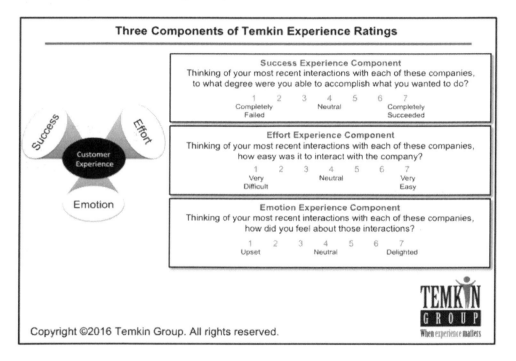

It is not at all evident that these are the perfect questions to ask in a study of customer experience. I don't dispute that they are valid questions. I would just find it difficult to explain and defend them in front of an audience.

Proprietary systems

Compaq and HP: The Account Loyalty Index

The Account Loyalty Index was a metric from HP and Compaq's deep-relationship survey and is now part of the HPE Relationship Assessment Process. It is a composite of three individual metrics and is an excellent predictor of customer spending. All three are on a 1 to 5 scale and they are averaged to come up with the ALI number. The component metrics are 'Overall satisfaction' (CSAT), 'Likelihood to repurchase' and 'Likelihood to recommend'. ALI scores of 3.5 or more always lead to increased spending. We loved the metric, though things gradually got more complicated. When HP merged with EDS, EDS brought its own composite metric from their Voice of the Client process. We never merged the two measurement processes, as they served different purposes. The EDS business was mainly long-term outsourcing contracts. VOC measured customers' views on the performance of individual agreements, while the Compaq / HP process was at the overall relationship level. The ALI and VOC metrics both took quite some time to explain to new audiences. The HP PC and Printer business had a different set of high-spending customers and its own different process and metrics. Once Meg Whitman came in as CEO, she found this all too confusing and imposed the Net Promoter System throughout the entire company.

Advantages and disadvantages

The use of composite ratings has advantages and disadvantages. The principal advantage of well-designed composite metrics like the Temkin Loyalty Index is that they should be better predictors of future market share than metrics based on answers to a single question. *The major disadvantage of composite metrics is that they are difficult to explain and understand.* It is hard to overstate how important that difficulty is. If you are not able to explain your metric in 10 to 20 seconds, I don't believe it will ever be completely trusted. Composite metrics all take too much time to explain. Unless the people to whom you are presenting work in customer experience full-time, you will have to start every presentation by explaining it again, as they are really difficult to remember. Too many audiences will start to doze off while you are explaining how the metric works. Those who have heard it before or who think they already understand it will just start to look at their phones or do their email while you are speaking.

59

Conclusion and personal opinion

The relative accuracy of composite metrics is irrelevant. They are close to impossible to communicate concisely and consistently. I therefore recommend avoiding them.

4.8 Journey Mapping

Journey Mapping is probably the most sophisticated and complete form of customer experience measurement and improvement. Perhaps too sophisticated. See what you think. Most companies and teams start off thinking they have relatively few customer contact points. They tend to think in terms of sales cycles. Typical terminology identifies these steps, all of which involve customer contact of some sort:

- Awareness: how a customer becomes aware that you provide a particular product or service. This could happen by a web search, sending email or paper mail, for example. Prospecting is another term used at this early stage.
- Qualification is where you discuss needs with a company to see whether your solution can indeed address their business challenges.
- Value Proposition is where you make a detailed proposal to the customer.
- Negotiating is where you address objections and additional requests.
- Close the deal.
- Implement, normally starting with a pilot project.
- Support what you have sold and expand the deal to other areas.

A reasonable approach for sales, not for customer experience
Selling is all about helping a customer to move through their own buying process. The proportion of people who move from one stage to the next is the conversion rate, and is a good predictor of sales success. The customer's experience with each step affects their willingness to move to the following one. Their experiences with other factors that have nothing to do with that step also matter, and are difficult to fit into a sales-centric journey map.

Incomplete and outdated
At best, this way of thinking is both incomplete and obsolete. Just consider the number of ways a customer can become aware of your product or

service. A friend may tell them about it via Twitter, Facebook or at a social event. They may read a LinkedIn article. They could do a web search and just happen upon it by chance. Their manager may just have joined from another company that uses the product. The software industry shows how the old way of thinking of customer journeys is incomplete. In the 'good old days', you needed to buy hardware to run software. This meant that the central IT and procurement people were important.

The growth of Slack is an example of a different paradigm. Small groups of users typically start to use the messaging product for free on their own. It spreads to larger groups that have the authority to buy the licenses on their own, since they need no new hardware, and it all grows from there. The history of Salesforce.com is full of stories of sales teams implementing the software without the permission or authorization of central IT. The message here is that modern customer journeys contain more potential customer touchpoints than you can reasonably map and address. Creating an initial journey map takes a long time, and it will be obsolete before it is complete.

Things other than touchpoints matter

The effort involved in creating a customer journey map makes it easy to think that the analysis covers all there is to cover. It is also easy to think that all touchpoints are equal. They are not. For most industries and companies, brand image attributes have close to the same importance as experiences customers may have when they contact you in some way. For some businesses, your perception as environmentally friendly or socially responsible can be critical. Think about the Whole Foods chain in the USA. How does your public image compare to that of your competitors? It is certainly more important than some administrative touchpoints like issuing credit notes.

Don't bother with comprehensive maps. Be tactical

Consistent with the rest of the messages about strategy in this book, I recommend doing customer journey maps exclusively for areas that have been identified by customers, partners or employees as needing improvement. This means you should do very few journey maps, and will probably only work on improving one or two at any given time. You do not have the resources to do everything everyone wants to do at the same time. Prioritize, using customer input. When people come to you saying they want to do a journey map for an area nobody has identified as needing improvement, be clear why you are saying no, and perhaps give them the opportunity to work on a journey map in a more important improvement area.

One situation where you need a comprehensive map

There is one situation where comprehensive journey mapping is essential, and that is when your company is replacing its existing management systems by new software designed to help customers and employees manage every interaction a customer has with your company. If you forget something important that your competitors have not forgotten, you will probably suffer. The customer experience team can help by supplying data about customer satisfaction with existing processes as you design new ones.

HP's software business grew through acquisitions, and we had many different ordering systems in place. When we decided to go for a single system, we used journey mapping to prioritize and understand the effort.

Exhibit 4.5

Customer Journey Map

Product	Pricing	Lead / Opportunity	Configure Price, Quote	Order	Fulfill	Licensing/ Entitlement	Billing/ Invoicing	Rev Mgmt. & Reporting	Support Services
New Product Innovation	Organization & Governance	Opportunity Management	Select	Subscription Creation	Service Provisioning	Customer Definition	Consolidated Billing/Invoicing	Rev Rec. & VSOE	Software Updates
Product Development	Analytics & Price Setting	Forecast / Pipeline Mgmt.	Configure	Subscription Configuration	Access Issuance	Rights Management	Credit Management	Report Revenue	Project Mgmt./Acct
Product Go-to-Market	Pricing Strategy	SW Try and Buy	Price	Order Management	Cloud / Service Brokering	Access to Support & Updates	Consumption Metering	Forecast Revenue	Training
Ongoing Product Mgmt.	Pricing Execution	Lead Generation	Structure	Credit Management	License Key Generation	Entitlement Reporting	Manage Receivables		Labor Tracking
Product Retirement	Technology & Data	Lead/Territory Management	Approve	Order Cancellation	Electronic SW Delivery	Compliance Monitoring	Collections & Disputes		Deliver support
		Partner Management	Generate Output	Renewals/ Terminations	Registration & Activation	SW Tagging / Deployment Tracking			
		Customer Engagement	Convert	Order Integration	Cloud Service Management				
				3rd Party Fulfillment					

Processes in **boxes** are significant customer touchpoints

Measurement and improvement systems

Based on the satisfaction metrics for the different processes, everything to do with ordering and obtaining license keys that worked correctly came out at the top of the improvement priority list. In addition to working on how to improve those processes, we determined how to eliminate the need for customers to deal with the keys at all. Exhibit 4.5 is an example of a customer journey map for a software company. There are items where customer interaction is rare. When using the map, you would use your own customer and competition research to indicate which items most need improvement, and which are the ones where you have a competitive advantage that you need to sustain.

4.9 Deciding what is best for you

While a number of systems have been described here, the one that is best for you may not be the one whose features and benefits you personally prefer. What follows are some additional decision criteria.

Your CEO's experience

Meg Whitman came to HP from politics, after an unsuccessful attempt to become governor of California. She had been CEO of eBay before that, and worked at Bain earlier in her career. eBay used NPS. Bain invented NPS together with Satmetrix. Nobody could conceivably have persuaded Meg that NPS should not be used at HP. She insisted that it be implemented across the company. If you have a new CEO and are implementing an improvement system for the first time, find out what the CEO used in the past and whether it was considered successful. Don't bother proposing anything else without a really good reason. Of course I am picking the CEO as an example of an important person. There may be others in your management chain who matter more to you.

Cost

If you have a limited budget, you may want to use whatever system costs the least, avoiding anything that carries licensing fees or needs substantial upfront investment. In principle, this would drive you to the Net Promoter System for general use, or Customer Effort Score for service centers. There is lots of free and inexpensive software available to support NPS implementation, somewhat less for CES. If you have just a small number of customers and want to get started with surveys, the free version of SurveyMonkey has certified NPS templates in a number of languages, as do some other companies. You should be able to find at least some NPS benchmark scores for your industry without cost. There are many online forums that discuss NPS and indeed other methods.

Measurement and improvement systems

Sponsorship

If you have done your research and found that customers are not currently mentioned among the top formal priorities for your company, you may want to pursue a highly selective approach. If other things matter more to your CEO at the moment, you should implement something that is easy to communicate, such as NPS, and run it explicitly as a pilot. There is an advantage in lack of current sponsorship in that you may have more time to gather data and prove the financial ROI before you are in the spotlight.

5. Types of customer research

5.1 Six types of research

"You would not believe how much we saved once we standardized decision-making."

The fundamental principle of any meaningful survey is that you must provide more value to customers than you extract from them. Don't bother running any of these types of surveys if you are not going to use the results beyond measuring your own people. For all but the benchmark surveys, it is critical to let your customers know you have heard them, what you have heard, and what you are going to do with the feedback.

Research types

There are six types of general customer experience research. A further type of survey gives important information about something that affects customer experience, though what you need to do with it is different in nature. Each survey type has specific uses.

Types of customer research

1. Benchmark surveys are used to compare your performance with that of your competitors. If the survey and measurement system are chosen correctly, the trend in your performance compared to that of your main competitor will predict your relative market share. Benchmarks can be done at the level of your overall brand, as well as for individual divisions, products and services.

2. Brand surveys are those where you ask your customers, partners or employees for their views on your company overall, as distinct from any individual product or service.

3. Relationship surveys are in-depth research with your most important customers. While they are a subset of brand surveys, they require a specific methodology. They are particularly useful if your company has a small number of large customers that provide the majority of your revenue. The best relationship surveys are done face-to-face by a customer experience professional from your own company. They are more directly useful than benchmark surveys in that the input can be worked on directly with your customers. Win-Loss surveys are covered later and are a subset of relationship surveys.

4. Product / service / project surveys get feedback from customers about one of your individual product or service offerings. Using the example of Apple, a benchmark survey would cover the overall brand, while a product survey would be about an individual Mac or iPhone model, for example.

5. Transactional surveys measure customer experience with various customer contact points. Examples would be satisfaction with a price quotation, an ordering process or with telephone support. While concentrating on the traditional approach, I will also say a few words about the use of mystery shopper to measure transactional satisfaction.

6. Supplier surveys are often neglected. Many large companies survey their own people about the experience they have with a list of suppliers. The company's procurement people are then measured on improving supplier performance in whatever dimensions are felt to be defective. If your company is covered by such a survey run by one of your customers, you are in luck. As distinct from all other survey types, the customer has 'skin in the game' and will want to

work with you on improvements. Syndicated supplier surveys also exist.

Now let us cover each of these in detail, plus a few words about mystery shoppers.

5.2 Benchmark surveys

The purpose of benchmark surveys is to understand your satisfaction and loyalty trends compared to those of your competitors. The key word here is 'trends'. No matter what your score, if your position relative to your key competitor improves, you will gain share compared to them. Done correctly, benchmark surveys will give you insights about how customers perceive your competitors as well as your own company. You will also understand which factors matter and which do not.

The top-level score in a benchmark survey is essentially a brand score; the overall perception customers have of your product, service and company. For companies with multiple businesses, benchmark surveys are done at the level of individual businesses, and individual products or services within businesses. No matter what individual product or service you may be trying to benchmark, the results are affected by respondents' perception of your overall brand.

While it is possible to design and implement your own, there are better ways. Forrester, Temkin and other research firms publish benchmark surveys. If yours is a large company, their reports for your industry will probably include you. If not, you can commission them or research companies such as Harris, IPSOS and Qualtrics to perform a survey on your behalf. This is usually quite expensive.

An emerging approach is for a group of companies to agree to jointly fund a benchmark survey. The best benchmark surveys are double-blind. This means that the respondents do not know who is funding the survey. The funding company also does not know the names of any individual who is answering the survey. While this eliminates bias, it also eliminates any possibility of follow-up. Most benchmark survey companies use panels of respondents that fit certain profiles. Panel members usually receive points or other cash-equivalents for their participation.

Benchmark surveys

Exhaustive and simplified benchmark surveys

There are two main forms of benchmark survey which I will refer to as exhaustive and simplified. In exhaustive surveys, customer views are obtained about all touchpoints in a customer journey. Lots of questions are asked on a consistent rating scale. They typically take a respondent about 30 minutes to answer for a single brand. There is also a single overall master score, often the Net Promoter Score. Factor analysis is used to identify the underlying factors. Multiple regression analysis with the factor scores as predictors is then used to determine which factors (and its questions) have the strongest relationship with the master score. Using factor scores reduces the risk of false positives and tends to normalize the distribution of scores

The main problem with exhaustive surveys is that *you are asking the questions you want to ask, rather than letting the customers express themselves freely*. Modern technology also means that the number of possible touchpoints has multiplied. Let's take a touchpoint example that may not be at the top of your list. Let's suppose you want to get customer opinions about the process you have in place for querying the invoices you send them. The customer might approach you by phone, email, chat or a form on your website, for example. Are you really going to ask the customers about their satisfaction with the response time, the politeness of the person they dealt with and the accuracy of the resolution for each of these channels? While the leader of the team responsible for invoicing may be deeply interested in the topic, it is doubtful that many customers actually care.

I have worked with exhaustive benchmark surveys for many years. The use of lots of questions with numerical ratings is problematic in that you don't really know why a particular rating has been given. You can only speculate. It takes a long time to complete all your speculation about your own performance. This is far harder to do for your competitors, as you don't know much about their work processes.

If your key competitor got a 5 out of 5 for some process where you got a 2, you don't know why, and you don't know whether that process matters to customers in any case. The result of this is that most companies spend no time at all analyzing their competitors' strengths and weaknesses, spending all their time on their own. "We are only able to improve our own processes, not our competitors', so looking at their results is a waste of time." is a typical response. Going back to the statements about business strategy at the start of this book, this is the same as a military general saying he does not care what the enemy is doing as he prepares for battle.

When using exhaustive surveys, it is normal to ask brand image questions as well as touchpoint questions. Factor and multiple regression analysis are then used to see which questions seem to correlate most to your overall rating question or index. When first doing this, I was always surprised by the contribution of brand image questions compared to touchpoint questions. Brand image items contributed about 40% in the HP hardware businesses and 50% for software. So yes, customers do care at least a little about recycling of ink and toner cartridges, even though that would never come up as a suggestion in a simplified survey. I cover brand image questions in the section on brand image surveys.

Simplified benchmark surveys

Simplified surveys have very few questions. An overall rating question is followed by "Why?" and "What should brand X improve?" For benchmark surveys, it is also necessary to ask panel members some demographic questions. For example, are they the decision-maker, a decision-influencer, an end-user, or a purchasing agent? What is the size of their company in terms of revenue and of employees? However, if you find that you never use these splits of data, you should eliminate the questions. The main challenge in simplified surveys is the accurate analysis of the open text answers.

The short format with open text answers makes it much easier for you to understand what customers like and dislike about your competitors and what they want the competitors to improve. You will make a difference to your company strategy if you can identify the top three good and bad points for your company and your main competitors. The high-impact items are the ones that differ among competitors, including your own company. These are what you should concentrate on in any communication about benchmark survey results.

High-quality comparisons are great for sales teams

Companies that have privacy policies all forbid disclosure of data from named customers. What this means is that you cannot use a specific customer opinion externally without that customer's agreement. However, double-blind benchmark surveys have no problem of that kind. You don't know who made the comments or gave the scores. You just know that they came from members of a credible and appropriate panel and were supplied by a respected market-research organization. You can therefore use them freely, though with care. There is a need for some level of diplomacy if you are a big company and have negative comments about a tiny competitor that you want to share. The truth of the comments could be obscured by a perception that you are being a bully.

Other than that, your sales and marketing teams should be delighted to have usable quotes and scores about your competitors, especially for areas where the quotes are positive for your own company and negative about others. You do need to be confident enough in the methodology and accuracy of the information to defend it publicly, if necessary. Personally, I have had good success doing this where industry analysts were taking positions about HP that were opposite to what I learned from benchmark surveys done for us by IPSOS and Qualtrics. For those in the IT industry, Gartner seems to be quite negative about NPS, so I open discussions with their analysts with the proof of the relationship with revenue.

Panel-based surveys are easy to criticize, but...

The quality of the panels used for benchmark surveys is easy to criticize. I have been surprised that vendors do not ban panel members who give verbatim responses like "I am just doing this for the points." or simply hitting the keyboard randomly "éoasdhfèoh". However, whatever the defects of the panel members and the survey methodology, the same defects apply to all vendors, so the defects probably don't make any difference. I say probably, because there is only one way to determine whether your benchmark survey is worth what it costs you: its ability to predict revenue.

Types of customer research

Relationship between revenue and customer happiness

The single way to determine whether your benchmark survey is any good is to determine the relationship between the master satisfaction score you are using and your revenue or market share trends. If your survey does not predict revenue, you are using the wrong vendor or the wrong measurement system. Exhibit 5.1 is a real example for a full set of large businesses. The relationship between revenue and relative NPS scores is the core item to study. (If you are using a composite metric or some other satisfaction indicator, feel free to test that too. It is really difficult to find competitive benchmark scores for composite metrics.) A relative NPS point means a movement up or down versus your largest or most important competitor. Since software has low barriers to entry and has many highly successful small companies, it may make most sense to compare your software to the average for a particular market segment.

Exhibit 5.1

Relationship between change in NPS and revenue

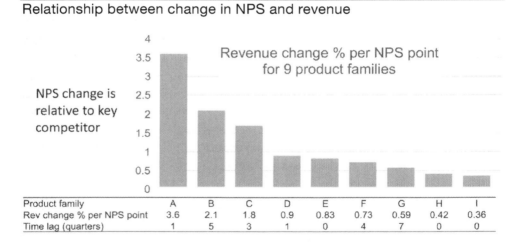

Product family	A	B	C	D	E	F	G	H	I
Rev change % per NPS point	3.6	2.1	1.8	0.9	0.83	0.73	0.59	0.42	0.36
Time lag (quarters)	1	5	3	1	0	4	7	0	0

Time lags

Just as changes in your marketing strategy will take time to have an impact, changes in customer happiness also take time to have an impact. In Exhibit 5.1, some businesses show a zero-quarter time lag. This is due to the three months it took to produce the reports after the surveys were carried out, so the effective time lags were a bit longer than those shown above. The low-impact, short-time-lag businesses were for easily interchangeable commodity products. By interchangeable, I mean that there was not much difference between our products and those of our competitors, and the products had low sale prices.

The harder it is to switch product or service, the longer the time lag. Think of someone who has just signed a seven-year comprehensive outsourcing deal with Accenture, IBM or HPE. No matter how bad the performance is, it is practically impossible to switch vendors in the short term. Think about a company that has just implemented SAP software to manage all of their manufacturing operations. The process changes they will have had to implement to adapt to the software are multiple and complex. It is very difficult to switch vendors. Finally, the impact of a change in satisfaction is higher for businesses with fewer competitors and greater product differentiation.

Revenue distribution is a potential shortcoming

Each response is considered equal in benchmark surveys. The views of a decision-maker have exactly the same weight as those of an end-user or a person who just has some sort of influence over the purchase decision. Since this demographic defect applies to all vendors covered, it does not have much impact. However, the views expressed by people from companies that spend a lot of money on your category of product or service have the same weight as those who spend much less. This is only problematic for competitive comparisons if your revenue profile is biased towards high-spending customers.

If, for example, you have a thousand customers, but get half your revenue from just forty of them, benchmark surveys may not be the best use of your money. You would probably be better off spending more on a relationship feedback and improvement process for the top customers than on benchmark surveys. It is of course possible to do demographic splits between different categories of customers, providing you have much higher sample sizes than you would need for an aggregated result.

Survey frequency

If you are in an industry that does not change much, you can afford to study your competitors less frequently than in the software business, for example. For heavy manufacturing or ship-building, once every year or two is probably plenty. For cloud-based software, you need to get as close to continuous real-time benchmarking as you can. Use cumulative-sum techniques and rolling averages to have statistically valid samples and still be able to adjust to change.

Presenting results

If you are presenting benchmark data to a new audience, always start by using a single slide or a few spoken sentences to explain why the audience should care. The slide should be the one that shows the relationship between customer happiness and revenue or market share for your company. If you do not yet have data for your company, you can find it for other companies in your industry from Temkin, Satmetrix and other reliable sources.

Exhibit 5.2

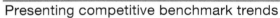

Presenting competitive benchmark trends

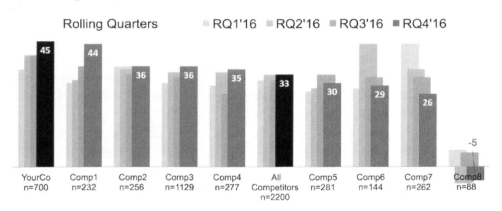

Since the financial impact of the survey results is all about the relative trends, you should focus on those trends when presenting. I have found overlapping bar graphs to be the easiest to understand. Exhibit 5.2 shows rolling four-quarter NPS scores. In this case, you can see that the overall competitive average has remained flat, you are in the lead, just, and your competitor Comp1 is likely to take share from everyone else. Comp6 and Comp7 are declining. Comp8's customers seem to hate them. If you have done simplified surveys, you should be able to say why.

People will react intuitively

As will be seen in the special section on Behavioral Economics, people will first react intuitively to your presentation. If their intuition leads them to an immediate easy conclusion, they will not pay any attention to the rational part of your presentation. The best way I have found of dealing with this is to start with a simple highly personalized story about one individual at one of your customers. You can even make up the story if needed, ensuring that any intuitive response it drives agrees with the insights you want to present from your data.

One final tip - never discuss statistical significance when presenting benchmark surveys

In my early customer experience days, and being a pedantic sort of person, I always included footnotes and other explanations about statistical significance on my slides and in my email communication. This was a big mistake. Here is why:

- It took time away from the important messages and made those message confusing. You want your audience to retain the trends, the reasons for the trends and what you propose to do about it. Add as little as possible to those core messages.
- Doubts about significance gave people excuses not to act. "Let's wait to see the next few quarters of results before deciding."
- In larger audiences, there was always at least one self-proclaimed statistics expert who would drone on and on, putting the rest of the audience to sleep.

The best approach is to ensure that you only present results that have an acceptable level of statistical significance. Mention this verbally at the start of your presentation, rather than providing details on your slides. If someone wants to discuss statistical validity in detail, set up a separate meeting.

79

5.3   Relationship surveys for top customers

In almost all B2B situations, you have a relatively small number of customers that provide the majority of your revenue. For many companies, it is not the old 80:20 rule, or even a 90:10 rule, but more of a 99:1 rule, or even 999:1. If you have a 'strategic account' team or something similar, you are likely to be in this situation. If you are not sure whether you have strategic accounts, a way of looking at it is to understand how many customers a face-to-face sales person has. If some of them are assigned one to three customers or partners, you have strategic accounts. You need to listen to them in a special way and work on improvements that are specific to them. Rather than going through a series of definitions, let me start with a personal story.

Shortly after HP and EDS announced their merger, I went to see Vodafone in Newbury, UK. They were a large customer for both HP and EDS. At the time, information from Vodafone showed that they really did not care very much for HP. My new EDS colleagues gave me their Voice of the Client (VOC) survey results for Vodafone, which were outstanding. I started the meeting by saying, "Look, I would like to cut this short. You hate us and you love EDS. I am going to learn what EDS is doing that HP is not, and copy it." The main Vodafone person in the room was surprised. "EDS is even worse than you," he said. "What makes you think they are any good?" I proudly produced the transcripts of the EDS interviews with senior Vodafone people. "But..." he said, "None of these people were actually involved in the EDS project." He then went on to give me the mostly-negative opinions of those who were indeed involved.

The message here is simple. Relationship surveys need to concentrate on the people who are most critical to your relationships with your largest customers. You should be really careful if you want to measure people based on the results of relationship surveys. If done incorrectly, they will find a way of cheating. Prior to being acquired by HP, EDS had an annual

Relationship surveys

trophy filled with money (a lot of money!) that went to the account team with the best VOC performance.

Relationships are relative

Some time ago, we hired a new account manager for an important Swedish/Swiss customer, ABB, based in Baden, near Zurich. OK, it was a long time ago, when Digital Equipment Corporation still existed. Being clever sorts of people, we at DEC decided to move a Swedish sales person down to Zurich. While ABB was based in Switzerland, the most important executives were mainly Swedish. We told him he could live wherever he wanted. He did his research to find out where the key ABB executives lived and found a house on a street near two of them.

He struck up social relationships, and was feeling pretty good about himself and his prospects after a few months. I thought he was fantastic, and that his thinking was perfect. One evening he met a sales person from Andersen Consulting, who was competing with him for an ABB project. They had a discussion over a drink. He asked whether the Anderson person knew Mr. X, mentioning that Mr. X lived just a few doors away from his own home residence. The Andersen Consulting guy replied, "Sure. I took his kids to school this morning." Oops.

Relationships can be complex

If yours is a large company and the customer is one of your most important ones, the relationship is likely to be complex. Multiple projects may be on the go at the same time. Some may be going well and others less well. One department can be ecstatic about you, while another may want to drop you as a supplier. Each person that deals with the customer in your organization is likely to have a partial view, but believe they understand everything. Good sales people are likely to know everyone that matters for their next deal, and may be totally unaware of an escalation on a product or service the customer bought three years ago.

Similarly, the support team may not know anything about a new deal that is being negotiated. When I was due to give a Big Data presentation to Swiss TV encryption provider Kudelski, I was given an exhaustive and rather

(Relationship)
(Based map)

painful briefing about a technical escalation that was in process. I was assured that the leadership team would not want to know anything about Big Data until the issue had been resolved. Once on site, the CIO did indeed note that "Our technical teams are working on an issue, but that is not why we are here today." None of the others present mentioned it, and we had a great session.

Who should be interviewed?

If your company uses Salesforce.com or Siebel, you probably have a formal 'relationship map', showing who the key people are at the customer end and who interfaces with them at your end, at least from a selling perspective. You may have an additional set of key contact people in your customer service system, and these can sometimes be people the sales team never meet. If you happen to be in software, you may have a Customer Success team with another set of contacts; mainly people using the software. Even if you don't have such systems, you need to establish a relationship map.

Exhibit 5.3

Tracking relationship survey results by individual

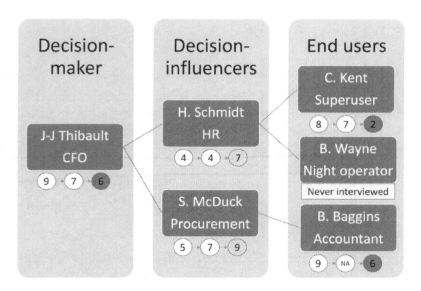

82

Relationship surveys

You can think of the customer's people in three categories: decision-makers, decision-influencers and end-users. They each matter to a different degree. This mix of people is the main reason I feel publishing account-level scores is a bad idea. You will just be kidding yourself if the decision-makers have gone negative about your company while everyone else has become more positive. You need to understand how the views of each key individual are trending. I suggest doing that using an organization chart. One thing you can see in the simple example in Exhibit 5.3 is that the night operator has never been interviewed. Trends for the last three interviews with the others are shown. If a person on this chart has been hired by your customer from one of your competitors, that is also worthy of a special note.

Customers should agree to the process in advance

If you have an executive sponsor system in place, the executive sponsor should explain the relationship survey and improvement process to the customer in advance. He or she should ask the customer to name a sponsor for the exercise at their end. The customer-side sponsor will be helpful in setting up interviews. Interviews should be done face-to-face, without the sales person or team present. Ideally, the customer should agree to work on the resulting improvement projects with you. The executive sponsor concept will be explained in more detail later in this book.

Who should do the interviews?

Not everyone can get access to every necessary person at the customer end. The most senior people may not want to speak to a customer experience person they feel is relatively junior. At HP in Europe our customer experience people were having difficulty getting access to some senior people at several different customers. We achieved breakthrough when the regional VP responsible for eight northern European countries said he wanted to do the key interviews in the Netherlands himself. He had no difficulty getting access to whomever he wanted. Other people continued to be interviewed by the dedicated customer experience team. If your company operates a 'future stars' or 'top talent' program, assigning one of these rising people part-time to a customer for a couple of years would be a good idea. This works especially well if the person does not normally have a customer-facing role.

Types of customer research

Interview format

A truly outstanding customer experience professional can handle 80 to 100 face-to-face customer interviews for a total of 8 to 10 customers per year. That includes writing them up, agreeing the contents of the improvement plan with the customer and project-managing the improvements. More junior people can do about half that, after their first year. Interviews as described below take about 45 minutes each. While I provide some suggestions here, it is important to pilot this and all other surveys before finalizing your own choices.

No matter what the level of the interviewee, I still suggest starting with your overall rating question, and that this should be the only question where you ask the person to give you a number. Then ask "Why?" In principle, it will take you three levels of "Why?" to get to something meaningful. Once you have suggested and agreed relevant actions, ask what the interviewee would like your company to improve, once again digging down to get practical suggestions. Where the suggestions are unclear, use questions like "How would I be able to know that this action was complete?" Most companies also seem to want to get feedback on the account team, so you can add relevant questions if the subject did not already come up. If the customer has not already listed the account team in the why or improvement answers, your team is at least OK. The overall message here is that the flow should be directed by the customer, not the interviewer. The interviewer provides a framework, and the interviewee provides the detail.

By speaking to lots of customers and testing different ways of starting the conversation, we have found one that works well. Try starting with "How can I make these 30 minutes into a good use of your time?" I have seen that simple question transform the customer perception of the interview from something that they just need to get through to a true dialog. It lets you understand what the interviewees' priorities are. You get the opportunity to bring them some value.

A totally different interview format

Probably the most effective interviews I ever did were with co-CEO Bert Nordberg of Sony-Ericsson, Manu Khullar, the CIO of STMicroelectronics and Julio Yepes, the CIO of BBVA, one of the largest Spanish banks. I filmed the interviews and got their approval to show them to any and everyone within HP. Rather than going through a standard set of questions, I gave them a magician's magic wand saying, "This wand gives you total control over HP. Make three wishes and I will do my best to make them come true." I had explained this in advance, and the level of preparation and thought all three put into the exercise was outstanding. Having the ability to show people the video that proved I was not making anything up was useful in getting things done, making most of the wishes come true.

Take a forward-looking view of your strategic accounts

When considering which customers to include in the deep-interview process, think a couple of years out. The most important question is how much the customer spends on your type of product or service, whether they spend it with you or not. If you have ambitions to grow your share with the customer, treat them as special now. In particular, treat them as more special than your competitors do. The relationship survey and improvement process is a good way of accomplishing this.

If you use resellers or other sorts of implementation partners, don't forget them in your relationship-survey process. Concentrate on the most important ones. If your partners also use relationship surveys with your common customers, see if you can gain agreement from the partner and the customer to share interview results and to work on joint improvement projects.

Communicating relationship survey results

Effective customer experience communication is always challenging, and relationship surveys are particularly delicate. Senior leaders like to see numbers, and I encourage you not to show a single overall number for an individual customer. Lead with the organization chart view, showing who has changed their opinions since the last survey. If it is your first time conducting a relationship survey, lead with the consensus list of improvement suggestions.

Types of customer research

If relationships are not quite that deep

If your customer coverage is not quite that dense or you simply don't have the resource or travel budget needed to go and see them face-to-face, the second-best approach is to interview them by phone, or a video link such as Skype. Just remember that the main work is not the interviewing, but the improvements. If your customers fit the 99:1 rule mentioned above, many improvement projects will turn out to be customer-specific. If you are closer to 90:10 or 80:20, you may find improvement projects that apply to many customers. In all cases, you must tell customers what you have learned quite soon after the interviews have been completed, then execute. Finally, if you only have the resources to do relationship surveys by email, I would suggest not doing them. I don't believe you can have deep relationships by email. You should worry if your competitors are better resourced.

Common objections to relationship surveys

Relationship surveys with large customers can be difficult to arrange. Contrary to what you may expect, the difficulties are almost always with your own sales teams rather than with the customers. The objections usually take the form of "I already work with my customer every day. I understand what they think and want in great detail. You can't possibly tell me anything new." These objections become stronger if you decide, despite earlier advice, to publish a score by customer. If you make the further mistake of deciding that these scores should be part of the formal evaluation of the sales leader at the individual customer level, you may as well forget about the feedback process. The sales person will prevent you interviewing anyone who is not ecstatic about everything.

If the account-level score exists and is (at least formally) not part of the sales team's annual evaluation, you can still have problems. One of our HP CEOs regularly read the interview reports for low-scoring customers only, and then phoned the sales representative to discuss it in detail. This did not happen where the scores were good. At one point, I wanted to get an account manager to agree to have some of his contacts interviewed specifically for software, not knowing that he had just benefited from one of these CEO calls. His answer: "OK, and I will do all the interviews for you. What score do you want?"

Relationship surveys

A sales leader's claim to understand everything that every key contact is thinking cannot possibly be correct. In our interviews, we have constantly been able to surprise sales teams by showing them changes in customer views, at the individual level, or that their preconceived notions about an individual are not correct. Customer contacts who have been vocal critics in the past sometimes turned into our most powerful advocates, if we listened to them and acted. As indicated early in this book, the problematic relationships are not the openly negative ones. At least they are communicating with you, and most want you to be successful. The problematic relationships are the ones where you have fallen into the deadly zone of mutual indifference.

Overcoming objections from sales teams

In a perfect world, you will already have other sales teams who have gone through the process and found it effective. You then use these first teams as references for the others. In the absence of such references, here are some suggestions, in priority order:

1. Be clear, in writing, that the sales person will not be evaluated on the overall score that comes out of the survey or on its trend over time. This can be tricky to word correctly, as it is not impossible that you will find bad chemistry between the sales person and essential people at the customer end. This might lead to changing the sales person. (To minimize the exposure to 'bad chemistry' issues, your account managers should be interviewed by the customer before they are appointed.)
2. Demonstrate to the sales person that you have the resources and sponsorship to drive the improvements suggested by the customer. This should be positioned as unburdening the sales team from the corresponding workload.
3. If you are in the customer experience leadership position, negotiate with the sales leader so that the customer experience lead becomes a formal position in the account team, accepting guidance from the sales leader. The formal description of the work should concentrate on the improvement process, and not on the gathering of the feedback. As customer experience leader, you should also agree to

function as part of the sales staff, and attend all their meetings, no matter where you report formally. These steps are designed to prevent perception of customer experience as a pure audit function.

4. Concentrate your messages on the individual people in the customer's organization chart when communicating feedback results. Your audience will find the individual stories highly interesting.

5. Involve the key sales people assigned to the customer in the feedback and improvement process. It may be easiest to start this when conducting a win-loss analysis, as described in the next chapter.

5.4 Win-loss analysis

"So why did we win?"   "Relationships!"   "And why did we   "Price!"
                                              lose last time?"

"And why did the
competitor win last time?"

Win-loss analysis is a subset of relationship surveys. You use the relationships you have within a company to understand why you won or lost a large bid. Many companies claim to do win-loss analysis but do it poorly. When we were working out why it did not produce useful insights for large deals at HP, we developed a better approach and applied it to deals over $100,000 in many countries.

Common practice and common results

Most companies do win-loss analysis in-house. By this I mean someone asks various people inside their own company why a deal was won or lost. Human nature means this approach turns out not to be useful. Worse still, you may think you are learning something, but you are not. Take the example of the sales teams. Where the deal was won, the most common explanation given by the sales team is that they won because of their outstanding relationships with the customer. Where the deal was lost, the sales teams most often say it was due to price. Each team in your own organization is likely to attribute some part of each win to themselves, and to distance themselves from any reason for losing.

Remember that a characteristic in B2B relationships is that your customers want you to be competitive. If you lose, they want you to do better next time, even if only to get an even better deal from whoever won this time around. If you won, they would like to be clear on exactly why. What this means is that your customers will accept your request to involve them in win-loss analysis, no matter which way a deal went this time.

Six-factor model for win-loss analysis

Exhibit 5.4 shows six competitive factors that should serve as a good starting point for your win-loss analysis. Ask the same questions to the customer and to your own team.

Exhibit 5.4

Six-factor win-loss model

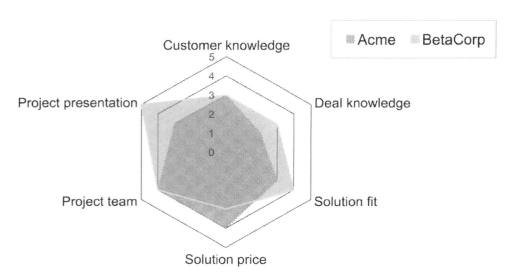

Win-loss analysis

Use this in try/buy product demo

The questions should be asked about your own bid and the winning bid when you lose, and about the second-placed bid when you win. Where you will learn the most is where the customer and internal answers differ most. Exhibit 5.4 shows a situation where a competitor won, and the key differentiator was the project proposal presentation.

You will probably want to discuss and finalize your own questions for each section. Here are suggestions for each area:

1. Customer knowledge *Industry* *Define market environment*
   - On a scale from zero to five, how well does each company understand your business and market environment?
   - How well does each company understand your business needs and challenges?
   - How good is the business relationship between each of these companies and your company?
2. Project or deal knowledge
   - How well did each team understand your organization's needs and critical success factors for the project?
   - How well did each company understand your decision-making process and make it easy for you to gain approval?
   - To what extent did each company help you define the requirements for the project?
3. Solution fit
   - How well did each proposed solution fit your needs?
4. Solution price *Price / ROI /*
   - How competitive was each price?
   - How attractive was the return on investment proposed by each company?
5. Project team
   - How experienced did you feel each team was with this type of project?
   - How would you rate the competence and professionalism of each team?
   - How available was each team to quickly answer your questions?
6. Project presentation

process ↓ decision makers board ○

91

- How accurate and complete was each project presentation?
- To what extent did the presentations give you confidence the project would succeed?

Adjust the interview format for each interviewee

The more senior the person at the customer end, the less happy they are likely to be with the use of a formal questionnaire. One approach would be to do your best to memorize the questionnaire and to take notes about the answers. I believe you can be totally open about the 'spider web' diagram that shows the overall positioning of your company compared to the best competitor. Try developing it directly with the person you are speaking to, perhaps using a whiteboard and photographing it when done.

Who should ask the questions?

The ideal person is the one who also manages the relationship survey and improvement process, assuming such a person has been assigned to the customer and works with the sales team. This is of course less likely to be the case if the deal is with a new customer, with no existing history. In such cases, use a person from your customer experience team, or a 'top talent' your company is trying to develop.

Reporting out on win-loss analysis

The customer should be first to receive your draft report, especially if you have spoken to more than one person. You may surprise them with the feedback summary and need to make edits. Your own sales team should be next, together with any partner you may have used for the bid.

From that point on, some caution is needed. There is no issue with sharing win reports with sales and general management. If you have lost, I believe you should leave it up to the relevant sales leader whether to share the report upwards or not. If the customer experience team distributes individual loss reports broadly, their relationship with the sales team will deteriorate rapidly. Aggregated reporting, covering many wins and losses, is the most diplomatic approach.

5.5   Surveys about a product, service or project

In this section, we will discuss surveys about products, services and projects. I include student surveys and employee surveys in the discussion. These surveys are all about your own offerings and do not gather information about the competition. You can execute them on your own or subcontract them. We have just discussed relationship surveys, and it is possible to view product surveys as being at the next level of detail. The lack of competitive information means they are not a substitute for benchmark surveys. Naturally, if you are a state monopoly, you don't really need competitive benchmarks.

It is all about what you should improve
When I worked at HP, we had a big gap in our improvement processes for large systems. We did not ask our customers' opinions about any servers, storage or software products, outside the anonymous benchmark surveys. We did our best to learn from things falling over, but did nothing to find out what to improve. We gradually reduced funding for our user groups, so they became less useful sources of input. Our printer and PC teams had a more comprehensive approach, at least for consumer products. If you bought a printer and registered it, you could be randomly selected for a survey on how you got on with taking it out of the box and installing it. Six months later, you might receive a survey to see how you liked the product and what we should improve.

Product surveys — the main challenge
Product surveys are the simplest in concept, and need care to execute well. For many companies, the main challenge can be knowing who is actually using your product. You probably have records of the people who contact you when they have a problem, but do you know who has bought and still uses your software, office furniture or industrial paint? If you only sell directly to end users, you probably do know. If you use resellers to sell your products, you may not have any idea. You may think you could just ask

your resellers to give you a list. If you also sell directly to companies, the resellers will be understandably paranoid about giving you the information. Of course, if your product must be registered to function, you can shortcut the resellers, but should you do so? Let's take the two situations separately.

Product surveys for direct sales

I was recently involved in a software product-survey for a product that requires registration and has existed for about three years. It is sold to small businesses. A quarter of the email addresses used for the survey bounced, and we were surprised. The quality of your customer list is important. If you have a list of email addresses but never actually use it to communicate with customers, you should not be surprised to discover that it is inaccurate. The message here, and for all surveys, is that who you survey is important. If you have an inexpensive product that is sold to small companies, surveying via email may be good enough. As you get to more expensive products, or have a subset of customers who have spent a bit more, consider surveying by phone. For high-value products or individual customers who have spent large amounts, go face-to-face.

In all cases, the purpose of the survey is the same. You want to find out three things:

- Does the customer like the product?
- Why do they like it (or not)?
- What would the customer like you to improve?

baseline of survey

Prefer open questions to long lists of things to rate

There are a number of different survey and improvement systems that can be used for this. Techniques for getting high response rates are covered elsewhere in this book. I strongly recommend using open questions rather than lists of things that you ask the customer to rate. Let me give a personal example of why. As a member of the British Airways Executive Club Gold level, I was sent a survey.

The survey had two main defects. The first was that it was administered by a third party who explicitly promised not to make my individual feedback known to BA. However, I wanted BA to have the feedback and to follow up with me. There was no way of doing that at the time. (The survey vendor and BA have fixed that particular issue since.) The second was that I wanted to suggest they copy a specific feature of the Swiss / Lufthansa equivalent program. There was no open improvement question on the survey, just a list of things to rate, most of which were not important to me. I was frustrated with the survey experience and left it with a worse impression of BA than when I started. I found it an interesting lesson. After all, the last thing a customer experience professional wants is for the research process itself to worsen the impression a customer has of a company.

Product surveys for indirect sales
It is really unlikely that your resellers will hand over their customer lists to you. Even if they wanted to do so, their customer Ts&Cs may forbid it. I see two alternatives. If the partner runs their own survey and improvement system, try to participate in it. If they do not, I suggest supplying your survey to the partner and suggesting a formal subcontracting agreement that allows you to run it for them. They can provide unique IDs rather than customer names to protect customer data.

User groups, internet forums and social media
—> check your forums : communities

Once your product has been bought in volume, people will start to discuss it online and to work with each other to provide advice and solve problems. This can happen under your supervision, via a user group that you form, or can be self-started by users. No matter how they get started, you should participate in these forums. If you can't afford to fund a person to do it, ask your product managers to spend an hour or two a week on the forums. Other employees should be free to participate, and should be required to add a sentence in their posts indicating that the opinions they express are their own, not the company's. If you mainly sell to large companies, the users may not be the decision-makers, but are important influencers. If the users dislike your product, having the lowest price on the market will not help you for long, no matter what the customer's procurement people may think.

You should prioritize these groups for input about future product features, and the most urgent things you should improve. A short open survey format will produce the best results. You should expect to receive lengthy responses from passionate people. Remember, the most useful improvement suggestions are likely to come from people who like your products most.

Once you have received suggestions for the next version of your product, let the user group(s) vote on them. Tell them the results of the vote, and commit to what you will and will not do. For the pedantic, Generally Accepted Accounting Principle (GAAP) revenue-recognition rules mean you can either commit to precise dates or commit to precise features, not both. It is common to list things that will be in the "next release" and in a "future release" without providing dates. Be clear about features they have voted for, but that you have no plans to implement. Clarity is more important than providing everything that everyone wants.

It is worth mentioning that studying your competitors' online forums may provide you with additional product differentiation ideas, though it is hard to see how you would survey that audience.

Unassisted forums are a bad idea

Apple is an example of a company that uses unassisted user 'communities' to support its products. When I recently bought a nice new iMac after 27 years away from the Mac platform, the initial installation did not go well. The website shown during installation for the software to migrate data from a PC did not exist. When I found it, there were two versions for different Mac OS operating system versions, but the installation routine does not say which OS version is being installed. I made the wrong choice and wound up with a 'spinning beach ball of death', requiring a hard restart.

Since I realized that tens of thousands of people installing iMacs in French must face exactly the same issue, I decided to submit the information to Apple via their communities, and via a site where you can provide product suggestions. I have heard nothing back from Apple after the submissions, though I note that they explicitly say I may never hear from them. If you have an Apple product, try searching the Communities. You get a large number of almost identical search results, many of which have no replies. Not good. They would be better off deleting the sites, since they are leaving the answers to third parties in any case.

Surveys about a product, service or project

Project surveys

Formal milestones are good survey opportunities for large projects while smaller ones should be addressed at completion. Best practice is to agree the interviewees before the project starts. Once the project is over, it becomes easy for the project manager to identify only people who have been positive about the project, biasing your results. Personally, I like to see the survey explicitly mentioned in the project contract.

The one theme I see come up consistently in project survey feedback is the need to have a single project manager in charge throughout the entire project life cycle, from presales through the pilot and on to completion. This is surprisingly rare. It is all too common that consulting companies (for example) put a senior person in front of the customer when bidding, replacing that person by a junior project manager who has never spoken to the customer for the pilot. Once the pilot is successful, the rollout is often considered to be 'mere implementation' and transferred to an even more junior person who has once again never spoken to the customer before. Not a recipe for success. For project surveys, in addition to the rating, "Why?" and "What should we improve?" questions, you do need to ask for the customer's views on the project manager. One way of putting it would be to ask the customer whether they would hire the PM, and ask follow-up questions from there.

Service surveys

Implementation services are a form of project and follow the same format. If you have services that are multi-year in nature without much change, you should use relationship surveys. Comprehensive or Business Process Outsourcing are good examples of services that should use relationship surveys.

5.6 Transactional surveys

Transactional surveys are by far the most common kind. They are the ones that fill up your email inbox. They are usually ignored, are easy to bias, give surveys a bad name, and are generally of little use. Did I mention I don't like them? There is a way to make them useful, and the concept that follows may be hard to sell within your organization. In short, you should only do transactional surveys in the context of working on your top five improvement priorities. I will cover the common ways of cheating at surveys in a separate chapter. Here is what you need to know about transactional surveys.

What are we talking about?
Transactions refer to touchpoints where customers interact with your company, whether in person, by phone, chat, email, your website, or other means. They can be about anything in the customer lifecycle that starts with discovering your product and may end with disposing of it in an environmentally friendly manner. The high-volume transactions in B2B tend to be about quotations, ordering, downloading something, web support, complaints, invoicing and contract renewal.

Survey immediately
You need to survey the customer while they still remember the transaction. I have been doing over a hundred flights a year for a long time. One airline consistently sends me their surveys about 'your latest flight' about two weeks after I have flown. I generally don't have any distinct memory of the flight. They ask whether it arrived on time. I don't remember. Were the crew attentive? Did they greet me when I came on board? How was the food? All buried in the deepest storage levels of my mind and generally not easy to retrieve. If you are trying to get feedback on the latest interaction, ask for it right away. Don't overdo it. I am constantly irritated by support websites that ask for my feedback as soon as I land on the page, before I have actually done anything. The pop-up windows are in the way. I am already irritated

that I have to look for support in the first place. Please don't irritate me further with things that delay my search for answers. Doing it when I seem to have found the answer is fine.

Follow up

Provide some sort of feedback to all survey respondents right away, at least to thank them. You need to follow up with angry customers right away. Don't leave them to simmer and share their bad experience with others. The follow-up call can be from the person who helped them, or from a supervisor. It can also be useful to have other people in the team make the call.

Only ask what is essential

Keep transactional surveys short. Continuing the customer service example, try limiting the questions to "Were you able to resolve your issue?". If the answer to the first question is yes (and only if it is yes) ask them to rate to what extent they agree that you made it easy to resolve their issue. This is the Customer Effort Score. If you are genuinely looking for improvement suggestions, ask for them too. Don't ask for any improvement suggestions if you are not going to tell customers what you will do with their suggestions. Do tell them why you are sending them a survey at all, and thank them for answering. If the customer interaction was necessary because something went wrong, take the survey email as another opportunity to apologize.

Company and customer views about when the transaction ends differ

I just want to give one personal example of an inappropriate transactional survey. As I write this, I am in the middle of my fourth attempt to get Air France to send me my new Frequent Flyer card. When I spoke to them on the phone three days ago, they told me it would take three weeks for my card to arrive. (I was not surprised as this is the fourth time they have told me that, but have never actually sent the card.) I received a satisfaction survey as soon as the call ended. As far as Air France was concerned, the transaction was over as soon as the call was over. As far as I am concerned, the transaction will be over when I receive the card. This is also common in software. A customer can contact you with a problem. After investigation, you determine that there is indeed a bug in the software. You promise to fix

Types of customer research

it in the next version. You then send the customer a satisfaction survey. This is nonsense. You have not solved the problem. The time for the survey is when the customer has received and installed the corrected software.

There are some common satisfaction challenges in supply chains

The Air France example leads me to the more general case of supply chains. Over the years, I have found physical supply chains to be the biggest source of disconnects between internal company metrics and customer feedback. Companies tend to discount customer feedback when their internal metrics show everything is OK. Companies are usually wrong when they do so. I want to cover three examples here.

Customers often believe a transaction has started before you do

I was in a memorable meeting in the Sweden with the procurement people from Ericsson about eight years ago. One item they brought up was that we were not able to deliver simple servers in less than two weeks. Our own numbers showed that nothing took longer than one week. Why the difference? I worked through a whole set of individual orders. A typical discussion with our supply chain went like this:

> (Me) This order took 18 days from when Ericsson ordered it to when it arrived. Why?

> (Supply chain person) No it didn't. It took three days

> Look here. They placed the order on March 3rd and it arrived on the 21st

> We only got the order on the 11th

> The date stamp is right here

Transactional surveys

Let me look it up... Ah yes, the second line item was obsolete

But this was ordered on our system. If it was not on our price list, they could not have ordered it

Yes, there was an error on the price list. We had to send them the correct part number so they could place the order again. They did that on the 11th

OK, but from the 11th to the 21st is still ten days, not three

You are not counting correctly. It took three days to clear the credit check, then there was a weekend. The factory took two days to ship it, so it left there on the 18th and arrived on the 21st. See? Three days!

!!!

Fortunately, these metric issues got fixed. Whenever you are dealing with anything involving a supply chain, you need to make sure the customer's clock and your clock start at the same time. All too often they do not.

Fill rates are often a reason for supply chain metric disconnects
Another subtler reason for disconnects between company metrics and customer satisfaction is called fill rates. Your supply chain people may be completely happy with their own performance when a 100-line customer order has been shipped 98% complete. At the customer end, the two missing items may prevent the other 98 working.

Types of customer research

Your leaders can pay too much attention to an issue they do not understand

I was in another memorable meeting about supply-chain performance in the corporate HQ of one of my employers. The subject was 'Deliver to First Commit' performance over the previous five years. The 'First Commit' is the first delivery date you promise a client. We were looking at performance numbers that had steadily deteriorated over the previous three years, quarter by quarter. However, their status remained 'Green' except after the first decline. The reason they remained Green was that the standard was continuously lowered to ensure performance stayed in the 'acceptable' range.

The head of the supply chain explained that he had only once shown Red status numbers to our CEO, and got "beaten up so badly that I will never show him a Red number again." The CEO monitored and understood cost performance, but did not understand or choose to understand the effect the lowering of cost had on delivery performance. The supply chain leader (I have to say that I understand this) chose to make his cost goals and "put makeup on the pig" of his delivery performance, lowering his standards to avoid 'red' numbers.

Supply chain surprise with Vodafone in Egypt - the partner lied!

We had issues with shipments to Vodafone in Egypt. Our business was indirect, meaning all orders came to HP via a local reseller. Vodafone told us that everything took a minimum of a month to get to Egypt. Our numbers showed that everything was fine. What was happening was that our own incentives made it attractive for resellers to group small orders into a single larger order. In the Egyptian case, the reseller was telling Vodafone that he had placed the order on HP, but had not. We were only able to discover this by working with Vodafone and asking them to email one of my team the order details as soon as they had given the order to the reseller.

5.7 Supplier surveys

Supplier surveys have not been mentioned in any of the many books and articles I have read about customer experience. I believe they are by far the most useful kind when they are done by, or on behalf of your largest customers. The reason is simple: these are the surveys where your customers have the most motivation to help you improve. They have invested time and money in the research and want to see a return on their investment. They may even have people who are measured on your ability to improve. There are two broad categories: syndicated research and proprietary research.

Syndicated research

Syndicated research involves people from different companies collaborating to produce a research report. A good example of syndicated research about high-tech vendors is the Gartner Global CIO Research Board. Members are global CIOs and former CIOs. Among other output, they have been publishing results of their survey about suppliers for over 30 years. For many years, the report covered just 15 suppliers. They have recently added Salesforce.com, Amazon and Google to the list. When Mark Hurd was CEO of HP, he was upset about our eighth place in one report. He asked EMEA sales leader Olaf Swantee (subsequently CEO of Orange Mobile) to take on an improvement initiative and I was the project manager.

We spoke to various board executives and members to ensure we understood the input, then put projects in place to address the top few concerns. By the time of the following report, we had moved from eighth to fifth place, which was progress. At that time, Cisco was in top place every year. We put a lot of work into understanding what Cisco was doing to establish this position. (Free test hardware and thought-leadership articles by third parties were at the top of the list. The article had titles like "Connected cities", "Connected government" and so on. They were outstanding.)

Changing priorities meant we had to stop the formal initiative. Our position gradually dropped over the years. Meg Whitman then picked it up and has asked various senior executives to work on improvements over the last few years. A feature has been the constant demand from the board for us to work with them on improving the results, and to participate in their events, including those on emerging technologies.

All good syndicated research reports give you information about the performance and perceptions of your competitors and more detailed information about your own performance.

Proprietary research

The first time I came across proprietary vendor research was with Vodafone's Supplier Performance Management program. While we did not get detailed comparisons, we did get information about our overall ranking and the areas they wanted us to improve. The important point here is that the people running the program for Vodafone were measured on improving supplier performance, so really wanted to work with us. The person running the program was then headhunted by British Petroleum to move to Houston and set up a similar program for them. BP and Vodafone are examples of companies who have invested a lot of money in their research process. You should find out whether your large customers have such initiatives and ask to be included if they exist.

5.8   Brand surveys

Brand surveys are those where you ask your customers what they think about certain aspects your company overall and what you should improve. They are not about any individual product or service you may offer. Of course, if your company has only a single product or service, there would be no difference. The surveys cover everything a customer may have to say about you. If you are specifically interested in the brand-image subset, there are reputable sources of brand-image benchmarks and comparative brand value surveys such as those from Interbrand.

Survey formats

Like benchmark surveys, brand surveys can take exhaustive or simplified formats. The exhaustive format with rating questions about all customer views on brand image attributes and touchpoints is particularly dangerous. Like benchmark surveys, you tend to have little information about which of the many items matter and which do not, so may waste resources on things that are not important. In addition, you don't know how you are performing relative to competitors. You may incorrectly think that an industry-leading but low score on something needs improvement. The most effective brand image surveys also use the simplified format: an overall rating question, a "Why?" question and a "What should we improve?" question. Since customers may not give unprompted feedback on brand image items, some companies follow the basic questions by an additional list such as:

"To what extent do you agree with the following statements:

- Acme is a brand I admire.
- Acme is a brand that has earned my loyalty.
- Acme has a great reputation.
- I prefer Acme to its competitors.
- Acme does good in my community.
- Acme is environmentally responsible."

Types of customer research

Brand image rating questions can be numerous, but tend not to be easily actionable. Since you are only asking about your own company, there is no particular merit in anonymity or use of a third party. If you are using email to send out the survey, the email should come from your CEO and promise both feedback and action.

A university survey example

Consider a Swiss university that wanted to understand the views of its business-school students. Using the simplified approach, the #2 improvement priority from students turned out to be earlier publication of the exam dates. At the point when the team considered using a traditional exhaustive survey, that question did not occur to anyone involved.

Employee surveys are an important type of brand image research

Employee surveys are common in companies that are too big for CEOs to talk to every employee individually. Most don't produce meaningful action that makes a difference to the employees. I believe the root cause is easy to explain: we don't usually use a simple way of asking employees what they think and what they would like to see improved. We have complex ways of going about it, involving asking employees to rate many factors on some sort of scale, such as from 0 to 10 or from 1 to 5. The surveys have so many questions that we don't dare ask employees to answer more than once a year. Typically, the results of such long surveys are compiled and published weeks to months after the survey takes place. Three things often follow:

1. Managers discount any negative input, saying things like "Things were special at the time of the survey. Several months have gone by, and things are better now. Let's wait to see what next year's survey brings."
2. Seemingly more positively, multiple regression analysis is used to work out what individual questions seem to have the strongest relationship with some overall metric, such as 'employee engagement'. Since we only have numbers, some sort of working group is then formed. This can of course just be a single individual. The task is to decide what can be done to impact the specific metric or metrics. The use of a single person or a small group essentially

discards all prior input and relies on the intuition (and bias) of the new person or team.

3. Common improvement suggestions such as pay, training or tools to do the job better, are not in the control of local managers. They then wait, and wait, and wait for improvements to be handed down from 'senior management'. Then the employees wind up giving the same input the next time, adding their frustration about lack of action.

Industry groups (such as ITSG in high-tech) publish benchmark scores, meaning the average scores for questions asked in a specific way with precise wording that all companies agree to use. The disadvantage is that this may lead you to focus on addressing those competitive differences, even if the particular question has no real importance.

Use the simplified survey process to get real-time feedback
Why not just ask the employees what they want to see improved? If you use an overall rating question for your company, followed by the "Why?" and "What should we improve?" question, your people will accept relatively frequent surveys. The short format also allows you to go to a more real-time setup. Why not ask 5% of your employees to answer the survey every week. That way you will quickly see the effects of organization changes, quarterly earnings reports and other things that may be going on in your company, country or industry.

Employee Net Promoter Scores present a communication challenge
Reichheld and Market have recently been pushing the 'Employee Net Promoter Score' or eNPS as a metric. It is measured by asking how likely the employees are to recommend their company to a friend as a place to work. Over the years, I have noticed something interesting about communicating metrics that are intuitively good or bad. In short, if a lot of things show up as having Red status in your report, it will be ignored. You may be trying to communicate that there are fires everywhere and that panic is appropriate. You will just get ignored.

For executives to be interested in reading and acting, the number of red items needs to be minimal. If you have a scorecard that lists twenty scores, two red, five amber and the rest green, you will be taken seriously. If your report shows fifteen red out of twenty, you will be perceived as insulting the executives and the operations they run. They will not believe you. At best, they will be polite and not tell you directly that they are not interested in what you are saying. This is where you can have a problem with eNPS. The scores tend to be about twenty points lower than the scores your customers give you. This means they will often be negative numbers. The minus sign in front of the number will destroy your message and turn people off. The best way around this is to concentrate communication on the answers to the open questions, rather than the score. If you must talk about scores, place the emphasis on the proportion of people who are Promoters, or perhaps the hopefully positive trend since the prior survey.

5.9 Mystery shoppers

Mystery shoppers are company employees who pretend to be real customers and go through at least some part of a purchase cycle with you. They are associated with consumer retail operations. In that context, they tend to work poorly. People in the stores make it their business to identify the shopper in question and share details throughout the organization. The mystery shoppers themselves tend to believe the low-volume anecdotal retail experiences they have are fair representations of an entire organization. Mystery shoppers have a place in B2B, though it may be best to use them for electronic transactions.

It is hard to see how a face-to-face business-to-business interaction could take place with a fake purchaser. However, it is indeed possible for web transactions. Modern B2B purchase motions include transactions that take place exclusively over the Internet. You can and should use mystery shoppers to test that such processes work. There are three situations where it is worth doing: prototyping, quality control, and feedback mechanisms.

1. Prototyping
Whenever you set up a new process for a web-based customer touchpoint of any type, you should test it by setting up a fake company and having that entity go through the transaction as though it were a real one. While that seems obvious, almost nobody actually does it, contenting themselves with the flow charts and software testing done by developers. You need someone with far less technical skill to go through your new credit-note process, or whatever it happens to be.

2. 'Agile' quality control
Modern software development processes can result in one or more software releases per week. No software is ever actually complete, and a new release may make things more difficult for your customers. If you are selling commodity products to businesses, increased difficulty at your end will lead

to increased market share for your competitors. Your fake company should be used to periodically check that existing processes continue to function efficiently. Cloud-based software that you procure from a third party will probably have frequent releases that you will not notice. It needs periodic checks too. Occasional paranoia matters for your most critical processes.

3. Customer feedback processes

I have been surprised to see people send out surveys or start to interview customers by phone without any prior testing of the feedback process. In addition to testing before you go live, your fake company contacts need to be on the survey distribution list if you use email. This is even more important if you use a third party to execute your feedback process. You should participate in their prototyping process and receive their live communication. Naturally your own responses must be removed from the final survey data set.

5.10 Fundamentals

The fundamental principle of all surveying must be to provide more value than you extract. If you and your company get value from a survey, and the customer does not, you should cancel that survey. If you are thinking of implementing a new survey and are unable to articulate the value that it provides to a customer, please don't bother starting. It is not enough to tell yourself you are providing value; you need to tell the customer about it too. Otherwise you are wasting the customer's time and giving surveys a bad name. Here are some fundamentals to bear in mind.

Follow up with people who give negative feedback immediately

Whatever your most negative feedback category is, people who score you there need to be contacted right away. A common way of doing this is to have the supervisor of the person they interacted with phone them. Having the person who provided service phone them seems superficially like a good idea, but it often goes off track. In short, at least some of the people will simply ask the customer to change their rating. End of problem for the employee at least. The supervisor, or a peer of the person who took the call are more likely to be able to treat it as a learning experience. A note of caution is that you need to prepare for the customer call. If the customer says that they have been waiting three weeks for an order they were promised within three days, you need to find out the status and correct delivery date before calling.

A category of feedback that deserves the same attention as negative feedback is lengthy feedback. Identify all responses that will have required time and effort by the customer. These customers have demonstrated their interest in your company, and deserve some interaction.

Types of customer research

Contact all the other feedback providers too, and even those who do not answer

I tend to respond to every survey I receive. I occasionally invent extreme answers to see whether anyone will respond to me. In the vast majority of cases, nobody gets back to me no matter what I write. Where they do get back to me, it has exclusively been in situations where I have provided extremely negative feedback. I believe you need to thank your customers for all feedback you receive, especially the most positive feedback, and let them all know what you are doing with the feedback. No exceptions. While I believe you should let people opt out from receiving surveys, I believe everyone who has not opted out should know what you do with your survey results.

And remember the 'couples' metaphor

Remember the metaphor about customers and couples earlier in this book. If you have a business that depends on long-term relationships rather than one-time purchases, you should use survey feedback as a great excuse for talking to the Passives, the customers where you have fallen into the deadly zone of mutual indifference.

If people opt out, ensure you don't send them new surveys

While this seems obvious, it is quite hard to implement in large companies. Your customers are largely unaware of your internal organization. If they have clicked on the opt-out link for a survey from one business, they expect never to receive a survey again from any of your businesses or functions. Make sure your opt-out process works company-wide.

6. Survey design

6.1 Considerations

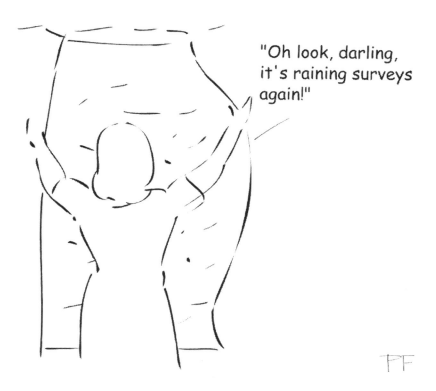

"Oh look, darling, it's raining surveys again!"

There are too many surveys in the world. Be selective. You don't have unlimited resources. Nor do your customers. Don't waste their time or yours. Here are some considerations that should help.

Don't ask what you already know

You will use your customer database to determine who to contact by phone or email. You already know who they are, so don't ask them their name. You already know what company they work for and what size it is, so don't ask. You already know what they bought. Use the information you have to demonstrate that you remember the customer. This is less common than you might expect. I have even been asked for my email address in a survey sent to me by email.

Challenging when you subcontract
When you ask a third party to run your feedback process for you, it is usual that the confidentiality agreements you have in place with your customers prevent you from transferring all customer data to the subcontractor. If you think this is simple, talk to your company lawyers. To be able to transfer confidential data to a third party, the third party must be acting as your legal 'agent'. This agency status automatically includes several other attributes, making it rare in practice. The consequence of all this is that the company executing the feedback process for you has to ask the customers for information you already have, wasting the customers' time.

Tricky vendor relationships
Survey service providers often work on a convincing pitch saying that customers will provide more honest answers to a 'neutral' third party. There are no studies that support this point of view, and I can't see why that would be the case. I strongly believe you should design and run your own surveys. A third party will never be able to understand the necessary product and service vocabulary as well as you and your customers. There is one exception, and it is competitive benchmark surveys, which must be run by a neutral third party.

Experiment with different survey questions
If, for example, you have thousands of customers for a product and want to solicit their feedback and improvement suggestions via email, randomly try different formulations of the email to see which gets the best response rate. Carefully test and measure the effectiveness of different survey questions. Test any new customer experience process in one business, learn from the test and implement improvements, before rolling it out everywhere. Experiment, experiment, experiment.

Keep it short
Keeping surveys short affects two things in a positive way: response rates and completion rates.

Considerations

There are many different factors that affect response rates, and survey length is not at the top of the list. The main thing that affects response rates is your relationship with the people on your contact list. If you write an email in your name to customers you know personally, you will get a relatively high response rate, no matter what the length of the survey. If you are trying to survey people who use a competing product and have never bought anything from your company, response rates are likely to be low. They have already proven they don't care much about you, so why should they waste their time?

There is no good, recent academic research on the relationship between the number of questions on a survey and the proportion of people who answer it, everything else being equal. It should be quite easy for a large company with a lot of customers to run an A/B test. An A/B test is where you try two things that differ in only one way. In surveying, this is done by asking half of a large mailing list to answer a slightly different survey from the other half. In the absence of such testing, you will have to rely on common sense and just trust that shorter surveys help response rates.

Exhibit 6.1

Effect of number of survey questions on dropout rates

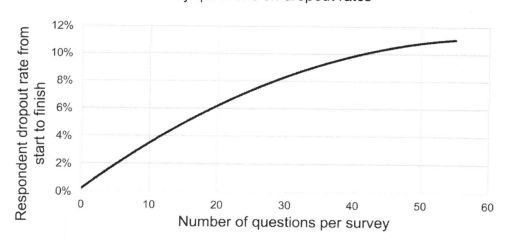

Survey design

For email based surveys, SurveyMonkey has done an outstanding piece of work to determine the effect of adding a question on what are called drop-out rates. A drop-out is a person who responds to at least one question, but does not complete the survey. SurveyMonkey looked at 2,000 surveys with one question, 2,000 with two questions, and so on all the way up to 2,000 surveys with 50 questions. Exhibit 6.1 shows what they found. Personally, I was surprised that so few people failed to complete the longest surveys. Still, the message remains that the shorter the survey is, the better the result.

6.2   How demographics influence research

It is tempting to keep surveys very short to improve completion rates and avoid wasting customers' time. However, I have yet to see a survey where demographics did not make a difference. Sometimes the differences are surprising.

What we mean by 'demographics'

Demographic information is that which you use to categorize responses. Again, you should never ask people to provide the categories if you already have the information. For web-based surveys, the categories you don't already know about are normally provided using pull-down menus. Examples are things like these:

- For product surveys, responses may vary depending on whether the respondent is a purchasing decision-maker, an influencer or an end user. Respondents are asked to self-categorize.
- For employee surveys, whether the person works from home, the office or is always on the road may matter.
- For a survey about a software product, it is useful to know what version of the software the customer is using. People using older versions of software may provide improvement suggestions that have already been implemented in the more recent versions. It is then easy to provide instant feedback and make them happy.

Gender matters

Even in B2B environments, women often provide different input to men. You should be able to do the demographic split well enough using people's names, if you have a few hundred responses. In HP's research on consumer printers, women mentioned ease of use and overall quality twice as often as men as a reason for recommending the printer. Men mentioned the price of supplies, low ink consumption and value for money twice as often as women. In short, the survey showed that women care about different things

119

than men. It changed the messaging and marketing we used, as well as the training given to people in retail stores.

An example from a student survey

A Swiss business school did a simple NPS survey among its students. Once again, women and men scored quite differently depending on where they lived. Women living at home were far happier than male students living at home. This was not expected. It was pure chance that the survey owner decided to look at gender as a factor. The full range of NPS differences by demographic is shown in Exhibit 6.2.

Exhibit 6.2

Student Net Promoter Scores by demographic

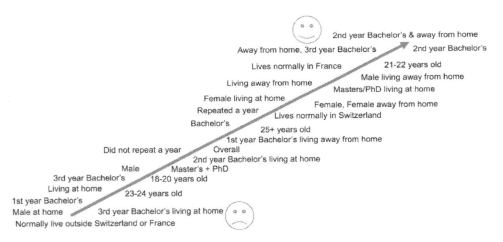

I suppose one other entertaining factoid from this survey is worth mentioning. While the beauty of the campus, with amazing views of the Alps and Lake Geneva was in the top three reasons students liked the school, half as many Swiss people mentioned it as French students. Too blasé, I suppose.

Action orientation

If you don't already have the demographic information but it is of no conceivable use in an action plan, please don't ask. Let's suppose you want to know what should be improved in your commercial air-conditioning products. Asking the respondents what age they are is of almost no conceivable relevance.

6.3   Ask relevant questions

An important factor in surveys is asking questions that let the customer provide feedback on what they think is important, not what you think is important.

The British Airways counter-example

As a frequent flyer, I have answered many airline surveys over the years. The British Airways survey process is the worst I have ever seen in any industry from any company. I am confident they believe it is wonderful, or they would have changed it by now. It certainly gives them plenty of metrics to use to beat up their teams. Exhibit 6.3 is a screen capture from one survey. These are the top-level summaries. The cabin crew section, for example, has sixteen questions.

Exhibit 6.3

British Airways flight survey – too many questions

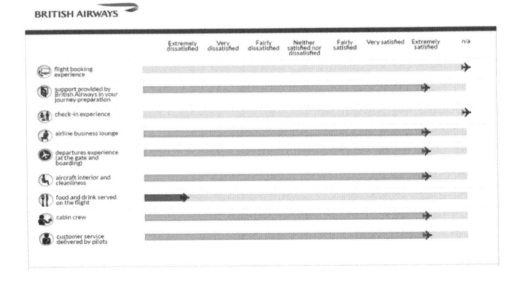

Ask relevant questions

The main issues with these types of surveys are:

1. If you are the company who is running the survey, you will tend to believe that each one of the 100+ questions is equally important.
2. No distinction is made between things that are hygiene factors and things that give you a competitive advantage. Hygiene factors just have to be 'good enough', and it is a waste of resources to make them better. While it is not an airline example, Rob Markey likes to use credit card approvals in stores as an example. You expect it to work. It cannot delight you. You won't notice it at all unless something goes wrong.
3. There is no screen where you are directly asked what you want British Airways to improve. That is the only conceivable way to decide which of these many questions actually matter.
4. The number of questions means some people won't start the survey and the drop-out rate will be a little higher than with a shorter survey.
5. The survey is run by a third party who guarantees anonymity, so there is no way for British Airways to follow up with you.
6. They do not provide any information about anything they have learned from past surveys or any improvements they have made. Putting aside the lack of possibility of individual follow-up, there is no commitment to tell those surveyed collectively what they have learned.

What should a good survey look like?
If I were designing the survey, here is what it would probably look like:

- First, the email, personally addressed to me, would read, "Dear Mr. FitzGerald, thank you for using British Airways for your flight from Geneva to London and onwards to Denver on October 22nd. We are trying to improve our long-haul service. We can see that you checked in online, had one bag in the hold that arrived with you. Fortunately, your flights were all on time, and the crew did not report any issues with the in-flight entertainment system. We would now like to ask you just four questions about your trip on October

22nd. The link below will take you to the secure feedback form. The survey should take you no more than three minutes. I hereby commit to tell you what we have learned from your feedback and that of other long-haul customers by November 30th at the latest. Now, please help us to improve."

- The survey questions would be:
    - How likely are you to recommend British Airways to a colleague or friend? [On a zero-to-ten scale]
    - Have your flights from Geneva to Denver on October 22nd made you more or less likely to recommend BA?
    - Why?
    - What should we improve?

I can't think why they would find it useful to ask anything else. If I don't mention the food and drink on the flight, they do not matter much to me. Note that the email is highly personalized and uses data the airline already has. I think the reason airlines often ask for the data they already have is that confidentiality rules mean they cannot provide it to a third party. Another great reason to run your own surveys.

7. Special section

How to cheat at surveys

7.1   Gaming the results is common

"A 10? I'm truly flattered. Now if we could just look at that 9 on Question 6..."

When your employees are measured individually on the results of surveys, 'gaming the results' is common and easy. What follows may seem a bit cynical, but has its basis in reality. If you are measured on survey results and want to manipulate them, here is how:

Transactional surveys:
*   First ensure the person you are speaking to is happy, then ask them to take the survey. This is probably easiest where a transaction is taking place by phone and the script requires the employee to ask whether the customer is willing to take a survey. Simply omit to ask

the unhappy ones. This can be risky for your service center people if asking is mandatory and all conversations are recorded "for training purposes".

- Sending system-generated emails with survey requests is common at the end of service center calls. If you have the authority to update customer records, and the customer is unhappy, simply change their email address before the survey goes out to something that is made up and will bounce.
- If you really need a bump in scores, replace the customer's email address with one that belongs to you. Answer the survey on the customer's behalf, giving yourself a top rating.
- Simply tell the customer that your pay and job security depend on them giving you the maximum rating. Car dealerships do this all the time, so it must work. Since Uber drivers and passengers both benefit from a top rating of five, '5 for 5' bartering is common.

How to get whatever result you want from relationship surveys:
- Only ask your friends at the customer or partner to take the survey.
- Pay no attention to their organization chart to find out who actually matters, favoring the people you have met.
- Decide who should be asked about a major project that has been completed only after it is complete. That way you can avoid surveying anyone who has negative views. Make certain to avoid specifying the people to be surveyed in the contract before you start.

How to game your company's product survey system:
- Only ask members of your user group or another enthusiastic club of people about your product.
- Exclude anyone who has a product escalation or service event in process from your survey list. Justify it by saying that you really should not bother them.
- Exclude anyone who bought a software product more than a year ago and has not updated to a more recent version.
- Don't do a product survey when you know there is any problem of any kind with the product. Wait for the problem to be fixed first. Use

vacation periods in another country or a long weekend as an excuse to anyone who wants to know why.

- Make sure the wording of the email or other request to take the survey does not use the customer's name, comes from a generic mailbox, is not in the local language, and makes no commitment to improve things. That way response rates will be lower. Low response rates tend to produce better scores because the people who love your products want to help you and will answer anyway. People who are less happy feel you have wasted enough of their time already and don't bother.

- Provide an incentive like entry in a prize draw for a shiny gadget to everyone who answers the survey. People won't believe they can win if they provide negative reviews.

Of course, if you succeed in cheating like this, nothing good will happen for customers, but at least good things will happen for your metrics, and perhaps your bonus.

OK, all of the above may indeed seem a bit cynical. I have seen all of these happen in practice. They are ways of avoiding finding out what your customers are thinking. The best way to avoid survey gaming is to ensure that no single individual who can directly influence the results is measured on those same results. Collective team metrics are usually fine. Ensure the purpose of your research is clear and that employees are motivated to help customers.

8. Make your strategic choices

8.1 Choose your strategy

Once you have a set of insights about each area in your situation analysis, the next step is to decide what you are going to do about it. Ideally, the choices will be a collective proposal from the entire team that did the situation analysis. There is a human-nature challenge in reaching a consensus in that people tend to believe their own area is complex and difficult and that everyone else's area of work is simple. Let me illustrate with an example.

We tend to under-rate other people's work
Shortly after I became the European software operations manager for Digital Equipment Corporation, we held a workshop with the manufacturing team, based in Galway, Ireland. Manufacturing reported elsewhere in the matrix. The enlightened workshop facilitator had each team separately draw a diagram of their own and the other team's workflows. The results were equal and opposite diagrams. Each team showed their own work area as a complex flow chart with many inputs,

133

outputs and transformations. Each showed the other team's work as a single box, either 'Make it' or 'Sell it'. Over dinner that evening, the manufacturing site manager asked me why the European business leadership in Geneva was necessary, since they (we) only seemed to prevent him going directly to market.

How to prioritize your choices

The best single method I have found for prioritizing strategic choices has two steps. The first is to vote and the second is an Ease / Impact diagram. A simple voting method starts when everyone present agrees that the definitions of the strategic choices are clear. Each person then gets three votes to allocate as they see fit. They can give all three to a single suggestion or split their votes. If there is a tie after three votes, give each person a further two votes. The result should be a draft list of five initiatives. Use an Ease / Impact diagram to validate the list. Exhibit 8.1 comes from a strategy session after a survey of business-school students.

Exhibit 8.1

Ease / impact diagram – top-right box is best

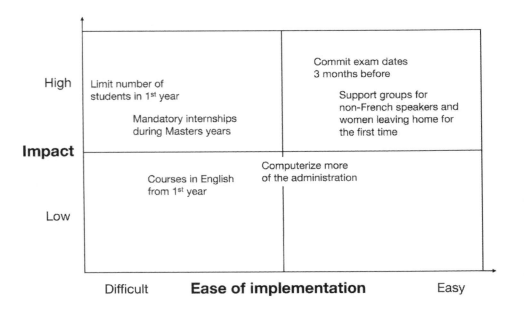

Choose your strategy

If all your potential strategic choices are in the low-impact high-difficulty box, you need to start again. If you want a more sophisticated prioritization tool than an Ease / Impact diagram, consider a criteria rating table. This takes some planning. You should agree the decision criteria before knowing what the list of insights is. It is too easy for people to reverse-engineer the criteria if they have a personal preference for which items are the top priorities. Exhibit 8.2 came from an evaluation of six different software solutions for automatically analyzing verbatim answers to surveys, compared to human analysis. The decision criteria are along the top, and each had a definition that was agreed at the start of the study, before any software had been evaluated.

Exhibit 8.2

Decision criteria and evaluation scores

	Access, read and extract	Frequency of topics	Recognize sentiment	Summarize	Filtering (refine report)	Present
Humans	5	3	6	4	1	6
Product 1	2	1	1	2	1	2
Product 2	2	4	5	3	4	4
Product 3	2	6	5	3	2	4
Product 4	3	5	6	1	1	2
Product 5	3	5	6	4	2	3
Product 6	1	2	4	1	1	1

Articulate your strategy

Since you understand your current situation in all important dimensions and have decided on the top priorities, now is a good time to articulate your strategy concisely. Customer experience strategy is a subset of a corporation's overall strategy and should be positioned as such. For example, if your company explicitly has no plans to grow its business, the customer experience strategy should not be positioned as enabling growth. Here is an example of a strategy statement, with associated initiatives:

- Our vision: customers for life.

- Our strategy: achieve industry-leading customer loyalty and renewal rates by ensuring every customer achieves the ROI they expect from our services.
- Strategic initiatives:
  - Implement Customer Success teams for our largest customers, dedicated to helping them achieve expected benefits.
  - Implement online and social-media user groups to involve the most passionate users and develop a sense of community.
  - Regular proactive outreach to all customers who do not contact us themselves and are not in the user groups. Ensure no customer is forgotten.
  - Catch up with our competitors in the area of free online training and how-to videos.
  - Catch up with our competitors in number of languages in our service centers, moving from the current two languages to eight, within two years.

The overall strategy statement shows a clear focus on existing customers. By implication, no new work will be done on using references to attract new customers, or on fixing defective products, for example. Outside the five initiatives, all existing improvement work is considered to be at least adequate. The five investment proposals may of course include moving people from an existing work area to do the new work.

Prepare for the investment decisions

If one or more of your top five priorities require no new investment in people or other resources, you are in luck, though that seems unlikely to happen. Preparing for the investment decisions requires hard work and good timing. For many companies, perfect timing means that the strategy development exercise is well-coordinated with the annual budget cycle. 'Well-coordinated' means the situation analysis and initiative proposals should be complete before the budget cycle starts, ideally several weeks before, to minimize surprises and maximize the opportunity to socialize the work.

Choose your strategy

Securing the investments involves understanding the level of sponsorship you have for your work, and how you will need to communicate it to each individual you are dependent upon for funding. Before covering that, we need to consider the overall role of employees in customer experience. Are happy employees necessary for customers to be happy with your company?

what is our CX strategy?
- Do we focus on current customers?
- Focus on new customers?

9. Special section

Employees - do they matter?

9.1 Conventional wisdom is wrong

Happy employee   Happy customer

It is obvious to everyone who works on customer experience that happy employees make happy customers. But… is there actually any evidence for this? Not much, though you would not know it at first. This research I am about to report uses a new method to study the relationship between the two, using public data sources. In short: happy employees count do not make customers happy. Nor do unhappy employees. Employee happiness explains less than 1% of customer experience variations across 336 businesses that sell to American consumers. I believe one reason for this is that many companies have no direct contact with their end customers. What this means for most businesses is simple: your customer experience investments should be concentrated on other things. To find out what things, ask your customers.

Employees – do they matter?

The pitiful state of research on the subject

Try an online search for 'Employee and customer satisfaction.' Most results are about employee engagement rather than satisfaction. As this is written, the top result is *Employee engagement: the wonder drug for customer satisfaction*[13], on the Forbes website. The author, Kevin Kruse, provides a link to a list of over 30 studies that are intended to be relevant. They make excellent points on employee engagement, which differs somewhat from employee satisfaction. However, only one of them contains multi-company deep research. More on this below. Other studies cover individual companies, including one on Caterpillar, and one on an unnamed department store, for example. Most of the studies listed make no mention of customer experience at all, but focus on other business outcomes.

Employee satisfaction and employee engagement are different concepts. Yes, more engaged employees produce better financial outcomes. Employee engagement indices are calculated as an average of answers to multiple survey questions. At HP, the employee engagement index was an aggregate of eight answers, including questions about training, processes and procedures, and ongoing feedback from management. There is no standard measurement. The Temkin Employee Engagement Index[14] uses three questions, none of which is about happiness.

The Forbes article links to research by the Northwestern University Forum for People Performance Management and Measurement[15] that is the only one of the list of 32 that actually includes deep and relevant research. The team studied 100 companies in the media industry. They did indeed find a statistically significant correlation between employee satisfaction and customer satisfaction for the companies studied. The R^2 number from their analysis was 0.08, meaning that 8% of the variability in customer satisfaction is explained by variations in the employee satisfaction data.

---

[13] The Forbes article by Kevin Kruse was accessed on November 2nd, 2016 and is here: https://www.forbes.com/sites/kevinkruse/2014/01/07/employee-engagement-the-wonder-drug-for-customer-satisfaction

[14] http://temkingroup.com/research-reports/employee-engagement-benchmark-study-2016/

[15] http://enterpriseengagement.org/pdf/employee_engagement_study.pdf

Conventional wisdom is wrong

Is the current state of research on employee satisfaction really pitiful? When discussing the state of this research in various internet forums, I am systematically told that I am wrong about it. When I ask for proof that I am wrong, I am pointed at articles that the person 'correcting' me has usually not read or understood. Indeed, as often happens in scholarly papers, the writer has read the abstract of an article they refer to, but not the full article. I don't feel this is the place to go into extreme detail on the subject, but would still like to pick one example, just to be clear that I am not making this all up.

A search on the subject quickly reveals a quite old Harvard Business Review article on *The Employee-Customer-Profit chain at Sears*[16]. The summary that others, such as Yingzi Xu and Robert Goedegebuure have taken away from the article is that 60 to 80 percent of customer satisfaction depends on employee satisfaction. The article does not say this at all. It says that 60 to 80 percent of customer satisfaction was shown to correlate with just 10 of the 70 questions on the Sears employee survey. None of the 10 is the overall satisfaction question (though "I like the kind of work I do" is on the list) and the HBR authors position the 10 questions as being a "management scorecard."

I don't exclude the existence of good research. I just have not been able to find it. I admit that some research is only available for a fee, and I have not been willing to go that far.

American Quality Digest article from 1998 put me on the right track

H. James Harrington made a lot of people uncomfortable in 1998 when he published *Happy Employees Don't Equal Happy Customers*[17] in the American Quality Digest. He used the American Customer Satisfaction Index[18] (ACSI) numbers for as many of the Fortune '100 Best Companies to Work for' as possible at the time. Only five of the Fortune list were in

---

[16] http://hbswk.hbs.edu/archive/801.html

[17] Part 1 is at http://www.qualitydigest.com/june98/html/perfimp.html
Part 2 is at http://www.qualitydigest.com/jan99/html/body_perfrmnce.html

[18] http://www.theacsi.org/customer-satisfaction-benchmarks

the top 100 of the ACSI list. Surely his results were a fluke, or were not logical in some other way?

My new data sources

At the time, Harrington used the American Customer Satisfaction Index benchmarks and compared them to the Fortune list of the best 100 companies to work for in America. The challenge is that the ACSI benchmarks cover consumer industries and a lot of the Fortune list are companies that are B2B, so are not covered by ACSI. I have therefore used a different, broader, and perhaps controversial source for employee satisfaction data: Glassdoor. We can debate the level of positive or negative bias that may be present in Glassdoor data. My working hypothesis is that the bias is equal for all companies. As the comparison being made depends on relative rather than absolute numbers, I don't believe the bias has any significant effect.

Exhibit 9.1

ACSI and Glassdoor for 336 businesses

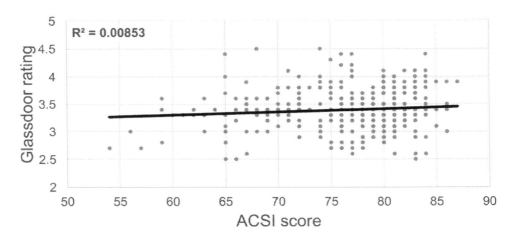

Overall Results

In short, there is a very weak relationship between employee satisfaction and customer satisfaction. I could match 336 ACSI ratings with corresponding Glassdoor ratings. Using linear regression, just 0.9% of the variability in customer satisfaction is due to employee satisfaction. For the stats experts, the number rises to 1.1% with quadratic regression. Exhibit 9.1 shows the results and gives an idea of the variability.

Exhibit 9.2

ACSI and Glassdoor scores for 117 'high-touch' businesses

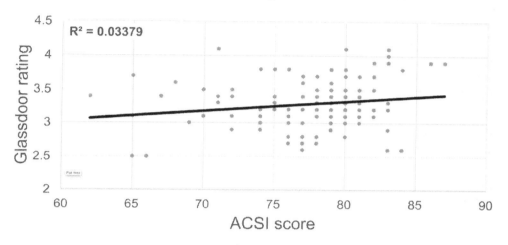

High-touch and low-touch companies

I used my own judgement to define some industries, such as restaurants, as 'relatively high-touch'. This gave a list of 117 such companies and these are graphed in Exhibit 9.2. I call the remaining 219 companies 'relatively low-touch' and they are shown in Exhibit 9.3.

- Using linear regression, employee satisfaction explains 3.4% of the variation in customer satisfaction for the high-touch businesses, compared to 1.1% for the low-touch group.
- Using quadratic regression, the numbers rise to 6.1% and 3.9% respectively.
- Whichever regression method is used, the message should be clear: for two-thirds of companies, employee satisfaction does not matter at all. For the high-touch companies, it matters far less than you might expect. There are industry segments such as hotels, where it

seems to matter quite a lot. The data file is available[19] for those who would like to do their own research or try their own high-touch / low-touch groupings.

Exhibit 9.3

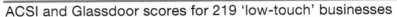

ACSI and Glassdoor scores for 219 'low-touch' businesses

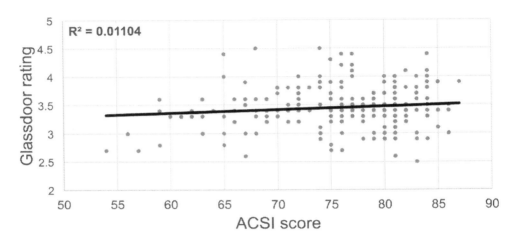

Not really surprising

I don't find these results surprising. Almost everything you read on this subject is anecdotal. It is easy to find articles on single employers who make both their customers and their employees happy. Nobel-winner Daniel Kahneman has written about 'What You See Is All There Is' as a common cause of misinterpretation. Where the only data being presented is on customer and employee satisfaction, humans jump to an unconscious conclusion that these are the only factors that matter. Surely things like product quality matter far more for a product company.

Most articles you read about existing research just present the two factors, leaving you to conclude that only these two are important. I am not going to say employees don't matter at all. They just don't matter much for the

---

[19] The ACSI-Glassdoor Excel data file is at
https://1drv.ms/x/s!AhvRy2CF3oochN5A7_0kaYu_nTG_iQ

average company. Think about the number of companies you like where you have no interaction with the employees. This is the case for most e-commerce interactions, for example. Amazon is an outstanding customer experience performer for e-commerce, but just about average for employee satisfaction.

Employee happiness can be driven by things like free food in the company restaurant, their pay, or the short commute a person happens to have to work each day. None of these do anything for customers.

One difficulty with the study

One potential objection to some of the data points in the study is that the Glassdoor data is provided by employees of the company, while consumers may only interact with franchisees or other resellers. This would be the case for General Motors brands included in the study, and for some restaurant chains for example. There is no known public source of employee satisfaction data for franchisees and resellers.

Conclusion and hypothesis

If you were to brainstorm a list of possible factors that could impact customer satisfaction, employee happiness deserves a place on the list. So do many other factors. In one such brainstorming session a senior manager suggested that the financial health of a supplier is an important factor for large corporations engaging in long-term contracts. I suspect it would be easy to come up with twenty or more factors that would bear scientific investigation. As far as employee satisfaction is concerned, my hypothesis is that it matters most in high-human-touch businesses. There is a major challenge in proving this. Many large companies outsource their service and sales call center operations, for example, so the 'high human touch' is not being handled by company employees at all.

employee satisfaction
≠
high-human touch orgs in the
cstm
Servies / Tech /
sysm
cstm

10.   Secure the investments

10.1 Four rules for enduring sponsorship of your work

There is no way to get funding for new initiatives if you do not have good sponsorship for your work from your CEO or other executives that matter. We often see business, NGO and public-sector projects, and even careers start with great fanfare, then grind slowly to a halt a year or so later. All too often, they disappear silently, without delivering anything. What follows are observations about projects and work areas I have seen succeed or fail over the last thirty years at HP, Compaq and Digital Equipment Corporation. The observations are presented in the form of rules that must not be broken. I have seen the first three rules right from the start. The fourth observation came as somewhat of a surprise during Léo Apotheker's brief reign as CEO of HP.

Rule #1 - Ensure senior leaders talk about your project or area of work
If senior leaders who have to approve new investments do not spontaneously mention what you are working on when they list their top five priorities, it will be very difficult indeed to be successful. This applies to all investments and indeed all jobs, not just those in customer experience. For the purposes of this discussion, 'senior leaders' start with your manager's manager. If your manager leaves, you are totally dependent on their manager for your project or work area to continue. Your manager's manager controls more resources than your manager does. If your work is not on his/her priority list, you will either not get the resources needed to make it successful, or you will lose the resources over time. I have not seen any exceptions to this rule.

If your company has an intranet, look for senior leaders' websites and study their priorities. See if you can find their typical meeting agendas. Is customer experience ever on the agenda? Of course, if they don't currently talk about customers as a priority, or their messaging is weak, you have a role to play in changing that, assuming you don't just want to give up.

Secure the investments

3 points to get weekend — 4/4/4/4 3/3/3/3 ou 19 #

Rule #2 - Make sure the project name makes sense

This should not matter, but it turns out to be essential in large organizations. The name of your project or work area must describe the work in a simple way. You should avoid code names and acronyms if at all possible. The following example is real, though I am leaving the description vague enough to avoid embarrassing people. One of the businesses I worked in had a major global customer happiness initiative called the Diamond program. It was well-funded and well-resourced, and had recently gotten off to a good start. HP needed to split up the relevant business to prepare for a major acquisition. The belief was that any costs held at the corporate headquarters level could be eliminated...

The cost review took place in a room of finance people, none of whom had detailed content knowledge of the cost areas in question. The following discussion was reported to me by two different people who were in the room. The discussion leader said, "... The next item is the Diamond program. Does anyone know what this is?" Since nobody did, it was immediately and irreversibly de-funded. That would never have happened if it had been called, for example, 'The customer happiness program.' The decision-makers would at least have tried to find out what it was.

There are times when things need to temporarily be secret. If your company is planning on acquiring another company, the project will have a code name until the deal is public. Similarly, your major customer experience project may involve an organization change and use a code name before it has been approved by the leadership team. As soon as the reason for confidentiality goes away, get rid of the code name or acronym and call it what it is.

Rule #3 - The work must produce something quite quickly

Sometimes I call this the 'pregnancy' test'. Yes, this rule has a slight lack of political correctness... If you can't deliver the project in nine months, don't bother starting. There will be no baby because you are not pregnant. Let me qualify that a little. If your first major deliverable worth the investment is more than nine months away, something is certain to change in the environment that will make you fail, or at least lose sponsorship. Your

152

manager may change. Their manager may change. The company may have a bad quarter, or a great quarter. Your company might get acquired. Your government department may have a spending cut, or a spending increase, or the balance of power may change in some way. I take this further in my work: you need to be able to deliver something every three months that is worth the funding and the effort for those three months. Otherwise you will gradually lose sponsorship. If you can shorten the time between major deliverables even further, so much the better.

Exhibit 10.1

The first three rules of project sponsorship

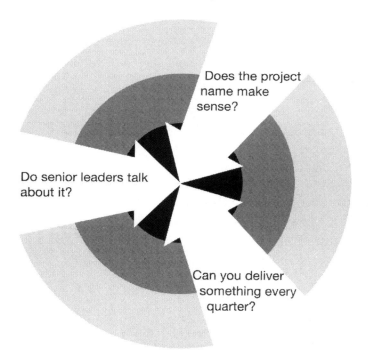

Rule #4 - Effective communication is critical

For years, I communicated these three rules, using the diagram shown in Exhibit 10.1. Then something happened that showed a dimension was missing...

Secure the investments

I worked with Léo Apotheker's head of strategy on the definition of our corporate strategic initiatives in a way that would make them easy for us to implement in Europe, the Middle East and Africa. I found both Léo and his strategy head, Martin Risau, to be brilliant thought leaders, with all the practical sense you would naturally expect from senior German executives. Indeed, when first discussing Rule #3 with Martin, he said "Three months is too long. We need to deliver something significant on each of these initiatives every two months." We had the perfect sponsorship situation: senior leaders were talking about the initiatives. They all had names that correctly represented the work. The initiatives would each deliver something significant every two months...

Yet we still failed. Why? I believe it was because we, and our CEO in particular, were not able to communicate the work and the results so far in a simple and consistent way. The story line kept changing. People became confused. Teams leading the work felt the work definitions were changing, even though they were not. I believe Léo was adjusting the story he told depending on his audience, normally an admirable quality, particularly if each audience can't easily compare the messaging with another audience. The extreme external focus on Léo's strategy meant the messages were compared, people got confused, and the work did not advance as quickly as it should have. Meg Whitman's experience in politics means that she has been able to avoid this pitfall. Her messaging was incredibly consistent, no matter what the audience, particularly during her first years at HP.

Conclusion

Sponsorship for your work matters. These four rules guarantee it. If all four are not in place, you need to get them in place or change your project, work area or employer. I urge you to consider the list as complete. Feel free to disagree. I would love to learn about a Rule #5.

10.2 Establishing credibility

When you are just starting up a customer experience team, you have to establish the credibility of both the work and yourself as leader of the work. This is challenging in many companies. Here is a method I have used to gain support for major new work. It was somewhat painful for me to learn this lesson.

f joined HP from his former position as head of Microsoft North America. He led HP's software business before moving on to be Chief Operating Officer. I was his Chief of Staff for HP Autonomy software while Bill led it part-time for a few months after Meg Whitman let the former Autonomy CEO go. Bill had an unusual communication and management style for the high-tech industry. I found it entertaining and intense to learn to work with him.

I worked hard to prepare for my meeting with Bill. I knew we would have several hours together and had prepared about twenty slides. After three, Bill became agitated and started to walk around the room. I started to see that he was envisioning himself on stage trying to explain my proposal to the 3,500 people in the Autonomy team. He was not happy. What I was proposing was far too complex for his stage style. He did not want something that was deeply intellectually correct. He needed something that was easy to explain. He kept asking, "What problems are we trying to solve?" We boiled everything down to two slides.

The first slide described the top five problems we were trying to solve. Bill insisted there should be no more than five. OK, I had to use 14-point text to get everything to fit on the slide, but still. The second slide had the same five rows with the problem names. It listed the leader who would solve each problem and what they would deliver in the remainder of that fiscal year (four months), as well as the new actions that would start as the new year began. The items for the following fiscal year mostly needed budgets or changes to sales compensation processes and metrics.

That was one of the greatest communication lessons I have ever received. Bill was an Executive Vice President. His messaging needed to be as clear and simple as reasonably possible. As people worked to implement the solutions to the five problems, they would add their own complexity. If the messages had started out complex, we would never have solved the problems. From that point on, I did my best to prepare and supply the most compact possible messaging to the most senior leaders.

10.3 Making senior leaders want to talk about your work

Sponsorship Rule #1 (Do senior leaders talk about your work?) is worthy of more attention. Let's suppose your senior leaders do indeed talk about customer experience, or at least quality, but it is not high up on their list. You still have a few weeks to go before these leaders will have to approve or deny your request to fund improvement initiatives. What can you do to improve the situation in that time? Here are three suggestions:

1. Prove the relationship between improving customer experience and improving market share.
2. Make it easy for them to talk and write about customer experience by providing them the material.
3. Invite yourself to their meetings.

Prove the relationship with market share

You are in luck if you have some customer experience data from your own company to work with. Many companies that have been surveying customers for years do not realize they have implemented part of the Net Promoter System. These companies already ask customers whether they would recommend your product, service or company to others. Customer satisfaction data is also useful, particularly if you have a large service center that solves problems for customers. Create a table that aligns the customer experience scores you have with each of the corresponding revenue numbers. Use correlation or multiple regression to show the relationship between the two. Test different time lags to find the best fit.

For product businesses in B2B environments, the best fit will probably come with a 12- to 18-month time lag. If you are measuring customer experience correctly, the relationship will be there. Remember that you also need to compare your revenue growth or decline with that of the market as

157

a whole. Your 2% decline can be fantastic if the market is declining at triple that rate.

If the first approach does not produce anything or you don't have the data, the only solution is to use external publications and benchmark data for your industry. This has the advantage that it provides information about your competitors, and the disadvantage that it will seem theoretical without any of your own company's data.

Make it easy for them to talk about your area

At HP I made it my business to find out who was writing relevant senior people's employee and external communications and website content. I supplied them with material that fit their website format, without being asked. It is quite difficult for professional communicators to resist customer-centric messages, ideally including customer quotes. Try it and see.

Don't wait for the leaders who will approve your projects to ask you to their staff meetings. Do what is necessary to get an invitation to present. Cover what your research has revealed, and what you think the priorities are. Solicit feedback from the staff and adjust your proposals to take the feedback into account.

10.4 Secure the investments

Once you have made your strategic choices, it is time to ask for the resources you need. Each investment proposal needs to have clear reasoning, including a statement about the customer and financial impacts.

Three categories of initiatives and investments

A good set of initiatives should include at least one proposal about work to be stopped so that you have resources to engage in new work. Prioritization tables can include work you are already doing and want to reinforce. In larger companies, it is helpful to think about investments in three categories and to position them that way when asking for resources. Indeed, the positioning is critical for clarity and to avoid falling into a typical corporate trap: getting the work and associated goals approved, but without any of the necessary resources.

Proposal category 1 — New work for existing teams

These proposals concern teams that report to the businesses and functions that participated in the situation analysis. The format is a proposal to do new work, securing the necessary resources by stopping specific existing work. Don't forget to include any training costs that may be needed.

Proposal category 2 — Shared central and local work

The second category includes proposals that combine people or teams that do not normally work together. Let's take the example of a company that has its headquarters in Singapore and an improvement initiative is being proposed for local implementation in the Philippines. The local team may propose that specific Singapore-based people be assigned to the work for its duration, working with the local people. Central teams usually react well to such proposals, seeing them as good development opportunities for people who do not get out into 'the field' very often.

Secure the investments

Proposal category 3 — New incubator teams
Truly innovative ideas usually involve new work that differs from what any team currently does. The general format for such proposals would be, for example, "We propose to set up a new customer complaints website and hotline. It will cover these five languages. We need seventeen people and $350,000 to put it into place by November of this year. The people will be in our existing call center in Amsterdam where there is sufficient space available. The experience of Acme company shows that this leads to a seven-point customer satisfaction improvement within 18 months. That in turn will improve annual contract renewal rates from 88 to 90% by 18 months from now, worth $3.2 million in annual operating profit. Sign here."

Make sure you have realistic implementation timing
In his book Thinking, Fast and Slow, Daniel Kahneman gives an example of unrealistic implementation timing. He describes his project for the Israeli Ministry of Education to develop and implement a curriculum for teaching judgment and decision-making at high-school level. The project included writing a textbook. After meeting every Friday for a year, his team had written a couple of chapters and had a "detailed outline of the syllabus." (I have difficulty combining the words "detailed" and "outline" in a single sentence, and this may be a sign if what is about to follow.) Kahneman asked everyone to individually write down an estimate of how long it would take to prepare a final draft of the textbook and submit it to the Ministry. The estimates centered around two years, varying between 18 and 24 months. These estimates turned out to be unrealistic, and the team had a way of knowing this in advance.

He then asked a curriculum expert in the team how long others doing the same type of work had taken. Based on his experience with similar projects, the expert said that others had taken a minimum of seven and a maximum of ten years, and that 40% had failed to deliver anything. Unfortunately, Kahneman's team, including the expert, considered this to be interesting but irrelevant data, believing it did not apply to them. In the end, they completed the book eight years later. By that time, the Ministry of Education had lost interest in the subject, and their work was never used. The message here is simple. Yes, it is a good idea to ask team members to provide timing estimates. If a team member has already done similar work, their estimate should be the primary basis for your planning, assuming you ensure they base their estimate on real baseline data.

Ensuring you actually have agreement

Early in my career, I sometimes left investment decision meetings mistakenly believing that everyone necessary had agreed to my proposal. Disappointment often followed. I found one reliable method for ensuring true agreement. This method tends to irritate the most senior people and needs to be used only when absolutely necessary. The critical slide in your presentation should be the last one, with the heading, "Here is what saying yes means." I realize not everyone uses slides for their presentations. Indeed, former HP CEO Léo Apotheker once told me "People who use PowerPoint have no power and no point." However, even if you use no other slides, this one is essential. If you are in a room with no projector, hand out printed copies.

Going back to the example mentioned in the third proposal category above, the slide would list the people, real estate, and other funding necessary for the project along with the timing and the names of individuals responsible for each point. You then go around the table individually to ask each person to say "yes" or "no". The first time I did this in one of the HP Software leadership team meetings chaired by Robert Youngjohns, he said "We don't need to do this. Everyone agrees." I insisted, and he quickly learned that this was not the case. It is in the nature of some humans to avoid public conflict and disagreement. They hope to manage it outside the meeting room, but it often winds up not being addressed at all. The downside was that my pedantic process irritated the team greatly, and I had to use it sparingly.

10.5 Communicating effectively

No strategy is worthwhile and no project is worth doing if you cannot communicate it effectively. Once the communication is about how your customers and partners feel about your company, intuition and emotion enter into play. Let's start with two suggestions. The first is on how to use color-coding of numbers to achieve what you want, and second is about use of 'identifiable victims'. Both are intended to help you to align the rational and emotional messages you want to get across.

Communicating performance

Consider the three sets of data in Exhibit 10.2 below. Let's suppose they represent your customer experience performance in different countries. The data is identical; only the colors are different. The messages are radically different between the first and second table.

Exhibit 10.2

Presenting results – avoid having too much 'Red'

Country	Index	Status
Japan	54	Green
Austria	41	Green
Switzerland	39	Amber
United States	36	Amber
Brazil	35	Amber
Canada	34	Amber
Australia	33	Amber
New Zealand	31	Amber
Philipines	29	Red
Spain	27	Red
United Kingdom	26	Red
Netherlands	25	Red
Mexico	23	Red
Portugal	22	Red
Turkey	22	Red
Belgium	16	Red
Germany	16	Red
Italy	12	Red
France	7	Red

Country	Index	Status
Japan	54	Green
Austria	41	Green
Switzerland	39	Green
United States	36	Green
Brazil	35	Green
Canada	34	Green
Australia	33	Green
New Zealand	31	Green
Philipines	29	Green
Spain	27	Green
United Kingdom	26	Green
Netherlands	25	Amber
Mexico	23	Amber
Portugal	22	Amber
Turkey	22	Amber
Belgium	16	Amber
Germany	16	Amber
Italy	12	Red
France	7	Red

Country	Index	Status
Japan	54	Green
Austria	41	
Switzerland	39	
United States	36	
Brazil	35	
Canada	34	
Australia	33	
New Zealand	31	
Philipines	29	
Spain	27	
United Kingdom	26	
Netherlands	25	
Mexico	23	
Portugal	22	
Turkey	22	
Belgium	16	
Germany	16	
Italy	12	
France	7	Red

Communicating effectively

If you are showing the first table to your CEO who has been in place for the last few years, the subliminal message is, "You have totally failed in over half the countries. You are a disaster for our customers." No CEO is going to accept that and your work will be dismissed as worthless.

The message to the CEO in the second table is, "You are doing a really nice job for our customers generally. There are some things to improve in France and Italy." That message is far more likely to be accepted. Remember the actual numbers are identical. The choice of red status is arbitrary, no matter what you think. Use red carefully, understanding its impact. The third table is a bit more subtle, showing a continuous set of shades from green through amber and red. It can be appropriate if your messaging is subtle too. We will return to this example in the chapter on behavioral economics to see how emotion can be added to change the perception of the same set of results.

Timing can change how you want to communicate
Let's suppose a new CEO has just arrived. The old one has been kicked out by the board for poor performance. Then there is almost no possible downside to presenting the first table, as the new person will blame his or her predecessor, even if you do not. Timing is everything.

Decide whether you want to emphasize or de-emphasize something
The leaders in the emerging field of behavioral economics have taught us a lot about how people perceive and react to different types of numbers. Our intuition and emotions kick in quickly, and prevent further rational thought. Rather than pretending it does not happen, why not exploit it? OK, yes, I am talking about manipulating your audience, but your audience is always manipulated; you just want some control over how and to what end.

Use emotion - Identifiable victims are essential
In his book *The Upside of Irrationality*[20], Dan Ariely describes an experiment run by Small, Lowenstein and Slovic. Two groups were given

---

[20] Dan Ariely: *The Upside of Irrationality*, HarperCollins, 2010, ISBN 978-0-00-735478-8

radically different explanations about humanitarian crises in Africa. The first group was given this text:

> *Food shortages in Malawi are affecting more than 3 million children. In Zambia, severe rainfall deficits have resulted in a 42% drop in the maize production from 2000. As a result, an estimated 3 million Zambians face hunger. 4 million Angolans — one third of the population — have been forced to flee their homes. More than 11 million people in Ethiopia need immediate food assistance.*

The second group was presented with a photograph and information about Rokia, a seven-year-old girl from Mali.

> *Her life would be changed for the better as a result of your financial gift. With your support, and with the support of other caring sponsors, Save the Children will work with Rokia's family and other members of the community to help feed her, provide her with an education, as well as basic medical care and hygiene education.*

Both groups were then asked how much of $5 each person had been given they would be willing to donate. Guess what? The Rokia group gave twice as much.

Customer experience victims

Applying this to customer experience, try not to talk about percentages and big numbers if you want to change something. Communicate it by video clips of individual customers, direct quotes from decision-makers, and talking through the journey or experience a specific person has had with your company. Make it personal. On the other hand, if you don't want to attract any type of emotion and don't want people to pay attention, use big numbers and percentages. As Dan Ariely puts it, "Rational thought blocks empathy." Humans do not behave like economists would like us to believe. Use that to your advantage.

10.6 Preserving your work in tough times

Most businesses have good times and bad times. Customer experience focus can be strangely counter-cyclical. A company can realize it is losing customers and want to know what to do. The customer loss prevents having enough resources to make any improvements the customers may request.

When I first got involved with customer experience at HP, I fell into one of these cyclical traps. The EMEA Managing Director gave me a European team of 150 people and we had started to work out a new strategy. A month later, I was told that the corporation had given the region a savings target. In the spirit of equity, everyone on the leadership team had a reduction goal, and my goal was $5 million. I had people and I had suppliers. I occupied real estate. I also had work to do. Somehow, it all had to cost a lot less.

My solution was still unpleasant and I ruined some people's lives, at least temporarily. I was determined that none of the customer experience work should be eliminated. We achieved most of the savings by renegotiating our ISO 9001 inspection and certification process with the British Standards Institute (BSI). I suspect they had already had to deal with similar situations. We were able to move some of the inspections to remote processes and to reduce frequency for entities that had performed well in past inspections.

We also moved a lot of work from Western Europe to Sofia, Bulgaria, where it continued to be done well, though at far lower cost. We were charged for facilities (buildings) per person, and those costs were substantially lower in Sofia too. While it was all unpleasant, it was good news for our customers in that our service to them did not change. I would love to be able to say that it improved, but it did not, at least at the start. It is hard for people to concentrate on improvements while they are worried about having jobs. My boss wanted me to be successful, and he also needed me to produce the cost reductions. If I did not produce them, someone else in the team would have had an additional task.

11.   Special section

Behavioral Economics

11.1 Behavioral Economics

Behavioral Economics is a relatively new field. It combines economic and psychological theory and reaches new conclusions. Economic theory holds that people always behave rationally, optimizing their financial and other outcomes in a totally predictable way. (I have always found this theory odd, even when I studied economics. It was never clear to me that the stock market behaves rationally since half the people 'rationally' believe they should buy what the other half are rationally selling. One half must be wrong, or at least sub-optimal.) Psychologists don't care much for the economists' view of the world, often proving that people behave irrationally. Behavioral Economics combines the two world views, giving us new insights about the way people, including your customers, really behave.

Key authors

The best-selling Behavioral Economics books are probably *Predictably Irrational*[21], by Dan Ariely, Thinking, Fast and Slow by Daniel Kahneman, and *Nudge*[22] by Thaler and Sunstein. Ariely has written follow-on books that I found less innovative. Kahneman won the Nobel Prize in Economics, mainly for his work on Prospect Theory, which is covered in the book.

System 1 and System 2

Kahneman's most relevant work concerns two different ways our brains function as we think: fast and slow. System 1 is the fast way and can be thought of as intuitive, jumping to conclusions on limited data. System 2 is the slow way that requires rational thought. He and his colleagues performed numerous persuasive experiments that show that the rational System 2 is lazy, and prefers to do no work at all, especially when System 1 has already jumped to its conclusion. I feel the existence of these two ways of thinking also explains most of what Ariely, Thaler and Sunstein have written. You may be familiar with a particular mathematical question that illustrates the difference between the two systems perfectly. It is called the bat and ball problem. Try to think quickly and answer it within two seconds.

- A bat and a ball cost $1.10.
- The bat costs one dollar more than the ball.
- How much does the ball cost?

Well? No matter what your final conclusion, a number almost certainly popped into your mind right away. Ten cents. Right? That answer is of course wrong. If that ball cost ten cents, and the bat one dollar more, the total cost would be $1.20. Appallingly, in large and repeated tests, over half

---

[21] Dan Ariely: *Predictably Irrational*, HarperCollins, 2008, ISBN 978-0-06-135323-9

[22] Richard Thaler and Cass Sunstein: *Nudge*, Yale University Press, ISBN 978-0-14-311526-7

the students tested at Harvard, MIT and Princeton got this wrong. System 1 jumped to the wrong conclusion while System 2 had a nice nap.

Relevance to customer experience

Customer experience publications and websites are full of System 1 content. By this I mean seemingly rational but wrong conclusions about cause and effect. My earlier chapter on the importance (or not) of employee happiness and engagement for customer experience is a great example. Most practitioners believe it is among the very top factors impacting customer experience in most businesses. It is not. We just jump to that conclusion because it seems so rational that we don't require any proof. What follows are examples of behavioral-economics experimental results that I found particularly relevant to customer experience.

11.2 Effect of what happens at the end

The Peak-End rule

What customers experience and what they remember are different. For our purposes, the most relevant cause of the difference is what happens at the end of any interaction the customer has with your company. Let's consider an experiment that Kahneman and his colleagues designed and called the 'cold hand situation'. Participants were asked to hold their hand up to the wrist in what was perceived as painfully cold water. The actual temperature was 14 degrees Celsius, 57 Fahrenheit. (If you don't think this is cold, get a thermometer and try it for yourself. I just did. Ouch!) The subjects were told they would have three trials, but actually only had two, in random sequence. In one trial, they put one hand in the water for 60 seconds and took it out. The other trial lasted 90 seconds and used the other hand. The first 60 seconds were identical. During the last 30 seconds, warmer water was added, taking the temperature up by one degree. The subjects were not given any information about what was happening.

Participants were then told that they had a choice between repeating either of the first two trials. 80 percent chose the 90-second version. This is totally irrational, as the first 60 seconds are identical in the two situations. 80 percent chose to have extra pain. This is not because they were all masochists. They were predictably irrational. What they experienced and what they remembered were different. In the cold hand situation, the slightly better last 30 seconds had huge weight, and carried the day.

So therefore…

From a customer experience perspective, this means that customers will probably most remember whatever happens at the end of any interaction with your company, no matter how painful or lengthy the overall experience. Let's suppose you sell a technical product and have just gone through a lengthy telephone diagnosis and resolution process with the customer. Let's face it, the customer believes the product should not have

Effect of what happens at the end

had a problem, so their attitude to the whole situation is not great. Rather than just saying, "Whew! It's running again. Thank you for your patience." make the call a bit longer. "Let's have a quick look at what happened next to other customers who had the same issue. Ah yes, here is how to avoid it in the future. And I can see that a lot of customers who had this issue also had this other problem. Can we take a quick look at that to make sure it is all working well?" Yes, it makes the call longer, but the end of the call is far more pleasant than the rest. Go for it.

11.3 The power of price

The lower prices are, the happier your customers will be, right? Not really.

One personal story

I found myself in charge of pricing software services for Europe at DEC. Customers had fewer problems with the more recent versions of our software, and we wanted them to update. First, we implemented a policy saying that once the software was two versions old, we would not support it anymore. That seemed to have no effect. Then the business leader, Denis de Pentheney O'Kelly, decided to add financial motivation. If customers were on obsolete versions of software, they needed to buy 'Mature Version Support' at a price premium of 50% over the standard support offer. In addition, Mature Version Support had a level of service described as 'best effort', with no guarantee of actually fixing anything. We sent this message to all potentially affected customers. Surprise! They were just delighted, and 100% took up this new offer, which they considered to be a premium service. Why does this make sense?

Expectations and perceptions improve as price increases

Dan Ariely and colleagues Baba Shiv, Rebecca Waver and Ziv Carmon ran a striking (and painful) experiment at the MIT Media Lab facility. 100 Bostonians went through the experience. While waiting, they were asked to read a brochure about a new painkiller, Veladone-Rx. The brochure said that in clinical trials "92 percent of patients reported significant pain relief within 10 minutes." The brochure also said the price was $2.50 per pill. The subjects (victims, in my opinion), were then told that the experiment was about perceptions of pain. They were connected to wires and subjected to a sequence of electric shocks, ranging from mild to very painful indeed. After the painful part, the subjects were given water and a capsule of Veladone-Rx.

Fifteen minutes later, Waver asked them to return for a second series of identical shocks. Almost all reported significantly less pain in the second round. It must have been the Veladone-Rx! Surprising, since it was just a capsule of vitamin C. In the following phase of the experiment, only one thing was changed: the brochure now said that the price of Veladone-Rx was just 10 cents per pill. Now only half of the subjects reported pain reduction.

In addition to the obvious conclusion that pricing has a surprising placebo effect, my conclusion is that behavioral economists are sadists.

Lest you think this is not relevant

My colleagues in HP's outsourcing business were very concerned. The CEO of a major multinational bank had recently testified to a US Congressional Committee. Included in his testimony were the words, "I knew nothing about any of my employees helping US citizens to avoid taxation." The bank wanted to be certain that this was true and wanted to implement what is known as eDiscovery software, and compliant archiving software to prove it. Ten companies were bidding. The bank's procurement people had told the account team that we were among the three most expensive, and had no chance.

The account manager came to me, pleading for a price reduction, having tried other methods. All our business with the bank was at risk, according to him. I asked him to imagine the following discussion between the CIO and CEO. "Hey Fred, remember that software we need to buy to ensure you don't wind up in prison? You will be happy to know I chose the lowest-price vendor." I asked the salesman how likely that conversation was to happen. He understood, and a few days later we were told who was on the short list of three finalists. Guess what? The three most expensive solutions were the only ones left.

11.4 Revenge

Dan Ariely had an appalling experience with Audi customer service when his car frighteningly stopped working in the fast lane on the Massachusetts Turnpike. They showed no empathy and treated him extremely badly. He decided to take revenge, among other things, by including the story in his excellent book The Upside of Irrationality. The question here is whether your customers will take revenge on you if you treat them poorly. The answer seems to be that they will, and it does not take much.

The Ariely Starbucks experiment

Ariely was self-aware enough to become interested in the nature of revenge and his desire for it. He used a Starbucks and an actor to perform his experiment on unwitting subjects. The actor looked for people who were alone and about to sit down with their coffee. He asked them whether they would agree to do a five-minute task in return for five dollars. He explained the task and gave them a sheet to sign, acknowledging that they had received the five dollars for the task. There was a small stack of dollar bills on the sheet which he asked them to count before signing the receipt. He left them alone while they finished the task, counted the money and signed the receipt, and went off to search for another coffee drinker. However, there were actually six, seven, eight or nine dollar bills in the stack. It was up to the coffee drinker to decide whether to keep the extra cash or return it. This was the control group for the experiment.

While explaining the task to the other half of coffee drinkers, the actor pretended to receive a twelve-second call from a friend who wanted to have pizza with him that evening. He did not acknowledge the call in any way to the coffee drinker, and just continued with the explanation after hanging up. This was the experimental group. The question was whether they would take revenge for the interruption by keeping more of the excess dollar bills on the table. And the answer is yes, they did. Rather disappointingly, only 45 percent of the people in the control group returned the extra dollars. The amount they received extra had no impact on this. However, when the actor had the fake interruption, it had a huge impact, and the honesty level dropped to 14 percent. Revenge for the annoying interruption.

The power of apologizing

Some time later, Ariely decided to investigate whether apologizing made any difference. He repeated the experiment, and added a third group. To the third group, the actor said, "I'm sorry. I should not have taken that call." just after hanging up. That one small step completely eliminated the revenge effect, giving results that were the same as for the control group.

Conclusion

You will sometimes screw up. You will sometimes upset your customers. Your products will sometimes not work. (Even a Rolls-Royce person is supposed to have said, "Our cars do not break down. They fail to proceed.") In such circumstances, the most powerful words you can utter are "I am sorry." If you don't... beware. Unhappy customers can and will find a way of taking revenge.

Wait, he told me to take $5 when I'm finished but he left me like $8, but then he was rude so maybe I'll take a bit more, or I could mess up the answers to the questions here but then I'd feel bad and probably give HIM money instead, or I could do both and just walk away with like $2, but what if it's not about the questions or the money, it's about the pen or something like that, I should check out the pen, but if I'm on camera and suddenly I'm this crazy person checking out the pen. I'm just going to do nothing and wait till he comes back. Maybe they're measuring how long I wait. I can't feel my fingers any more. Should I smile a little? I wish I could move. Maybe now he's afraid to come back. Are they closing?

11.5 Nudging customers to do what they should

In their book *Nudge*, Richard Thaler and Cass Sunstein explain that people are poor at choosing among options, and can quite easily be 'nudged' or pushed gently to make a specific choice. They promote the concept of 'Libertarian Paternalism', encouraging leaders to nudge all of us in directions that give us the greatest long-term benefit. There is a single important principle that permeates their work: humans need well-chosen default options for their major and minor choices in life and as consumers. They also need to be able to change the default choice.

Libertarian paternalism

The authors give an example of what they mean using the experience of employees at the University of Chicago. They have a subsidized health plan that comes up for renewal each year. They receive paper and email information about the available plans well before the renewal deadline. The question is what should happen when the employee forgets to renew. Should the default be, for example, to continue the prior year's plan, or to reset them to having no health plan. Except for the economically desperate, it seems unlikely that anyone would reasonably want to cancel their (say) $1,000 per month family health plan that is matched by equal funding from their employer. Libertarian paternalism suggests that the default choice, preselected in the online form, should be to continue the current plan.

Relevance

All companies and government institutions present their customers with choices. The companies providing the choices have a much deeper understanding of the consequences of the choices than the customers do. This is where companies can and must actively suggest the choices customers should make, rather than leaving them with a list to choose from. Assuming the statement is true, a way of handling the issue would be to say, "most customers like you choose this option." I suggest being more active.

Nudging customers to do what they should

Retail bank example

Consider the example of hardware maintenance for a retail bank's infrastructure. Let's suppose we are only talking about what they need to run the front office while the physical bank is open, from Monday to Friday. I remember an example from DEC where a UK bank had contracted to have a one-hour on-site support service, Monday to Friday, in working hours. That seemed quite logical until a disk failed in a RAID array. These are massively redundant, and failed disks do not need immediate replacement. One of our people was at their office within 30 minutes. The customer said they could not deal with this during working hours, and asked them to come back the following day, a Saturday. They did not have a contract for this. With a bit more thought, our default option for retail banks could and should have been 24x7 service. We wrongly thought we should just give them a set of choices, and they chose the one that cost the least. We should have used our experience with other banks to nudge them to a better default, even though it would cost them more.

11.6 Adding emotion to numbers

It is quite easy to add emotion to numbers. Adding it changes how people react to them.

An energy reduction experiment

In *Nudge* the authors describe an experiment run by Schultz and colleagues in San Marcos, California in 2007. The experiment was about household energy reduction. About 300 households were given information about their energy consumption in the previous weeks. They were also given accurate information about the average consumption across all households. However, half were just given the numbers, and half were given the numbers, plus a smiley face if they were below the average and an unhappy face if they consumed more than the average. The difference in subsequent behavior between the two groups was remarkable. Households with below-average consumption who were given just the numbers increased their consumption over the following months. Those who additionally had a smiley face on their report did not increase consumption. While both above-average groups decreased their consumption, the decrease was considerably more for those who received an unhappy emoticon on their reports.

There are everyday examples

I have noticed the same phenomenon with local information-only speed traps here in Switzerland. One quite close to where I live has an emoticon after the speed number. I am always happy when I see a green smiley face. With other non-emoticon displays, if I see that I am quite a bit below the limit, I tend to speed up.

For customer experience reporting

What this means is that you should carefully and selectively add emoticons to your reporting. Gender-related perceptions exist, and you may want to be particularly careful when first using this if you are female. One sexist remark I heard was, "Next she will be dotting her 'I's with a little heart." That notwithstanding, I want to add emotion to the numbers I used when discussing effective communication. In Exhibit 11.1 below, the first two sets of data are the same as in Exhibit 10.2 above. I have added a new one where the emphasis is on the trend. In every customer experience metric I can think of, and indeed in most operational metrics, the trend is far more important than the absolute number. Adding the trend smileys changes the message completely. Now we finally understand that Canada and Portugal are the countries that most need additional focus. France and Italy may have poor absolute numbers, but they are making progress. Once again, executives will only take this type of message seriously if you have very few red status items. You should treat red as a relative status, rather than relying on absolute numbers.

Exhibit 11.1

Adding emotion to scorecards

Country	Index	Status	Country	Index	Status	Country	Index	Status	Trend
Japan	54	Green	Japan	54	Green	Japan	54	Green	☺
Austria	41	Green	Austria	41	Green	Austria	41	Green	☺
Switzerland	39	Amber	Switzerland	39	Green	Switzerland	39	Green	☺
United States	36	Amber	United States	36	Green	United States	36	Green	☹
Brazil	35	Amber	Brazil	35	Green	Brazil	35	Green	☺
Canada	34	Amber	Canada	34	Green	Canada	34	Green	☹
Australia	33	Amber	Australia	33	Green	Australia	33	Green	☺
New Zealand	31	Amber	New Zealand	31	Green	New Zealand	31	Green	☺
Philipines	29	Red	Philipines	29	Green	Philipines	29	Green	☺
Spain	27	Red	Spain	27	Green	Spain	27	Green	☺
United Kingdom	26	Red	United Kingdom	26	Green	United Kingdom	26	Green	☺
Netherlands	25	Red	Netherlands	25	Amber	Netherlands	25	Amber	☺
Mexico	23	Red	Mexico	23	Amber	Mexico	23	Amber	☹
Portugal	22	Red	Portugal	22	Amber	Portugal	22	Amber	☹
Turkey	22	Red	Turkey	22	Amber	Turkey	22	Amber	☺
Belgium	16	Red	Belgium	16	Amber	Belgium	16	Amber	☺
Germany	16	Red	Germany	16	Amber	Germany	16	Amber	☺
Italy	12	Red	Italy	12	Red	Italy	12	Red	☺
France	7	Red	France	7	Red	France	7	Red	☺

11.7 Denominator neglect

Psychologists have often repeated the following experiment. Participants are given a choice of drawing marbles from one of two urns, in which red marbles win a prize. They are told how many white and red marbles are in each urn:

- Urn A contains 10 marbles, of which is one is red.
- Urn B contains 100 marbles, of which eight are red.

Easy, right? Not so. In the various repetitions of the experiment, 30 to 40% of students chose Urn B, despite the lower probability of winning.

The average person is very bad at math

As Kahneman notes, "…the remarkably foolish choices that people make in this situation have attracted the attention of many researchers." He uses Paul Slovic's term denominator neglect to describe it. Some of the phenomenon seems to be explained by how vivid the image of something is in our minds. It is easy for us to imagine the eight winning red marbles against a rather indistinct background of white. Our System 1 has acted, and found the answer. System 2 continues to take a nap. Perhaps more remarkably, one study showed that people told about a disease that "kills 1,286 people out of every 10,000" believed it to be more dangerous than "a disease that kills 24.14% of the population." The imagery of the absolute number overwhelms the relatively abstract notion of a percentage.

This matters for how you communicate the results of any study of what customers want. When you want your audience to internalize and act based on your numbers, use absolute numbers, not percentages. You will of course occasionally want people not to pay much attention to some numbers, and the use of percentages will help. Paul Slovic and his colleagues cite an article that states that "approximately 1,000 homicides a year are committed nationwide by seriously mentally ill individuals who are not taking their medication." That could also accurately be expressed as "the annual likelihood of being killed by such an individual is approximately 0.00036%." The former grabs your attention on an emotional topic. The latter makes you want to yawn. The version to use depends on what you want to accomplish.

12. Implement and experiment

12.1 Implement and experiment

A more complete title would be 'Experiment and implement and experiment'. Once you have approval to move ahead, piloting or prototyping anything new is essential. This is particularly important if it touches your customers. You want the new tools and processes to be robust before you implement them for all your customers. This is not a book about project management, though a few typical project-management approaches are worth noting.

Kickoff

Hold your first implementation meeting face-to-face. This is particularly important in large organizations with people in multiple locations. Trust is established far more quickly when you can look someone in the eyes. If you are in a large company, I am sure you will have witnessed colleagues who freely criticize those they have never met. It is much rarer when people get to know each other. Ideally, when kicking off the set of new initiatives, you should have the project teams for all approved projects get together. The primary purpose of the first workshop is to produce the first task plan; the list of work, deliverables, resources, timing and interdependencies for each initiative. The teams should also address completion criteria and risk management and do some simple 'speed dating'.

Implement and experiment

Risk management

As you set out our implementation plan, try to brainstorm everything that could go wrong, then document what you will do when it goes wrong. Some examples might be:

- The company has a bad quarter and you lose the funding you need to complete the project properly.
- The manager who approved your project leaves the company.
- The software you are developing takes much longer than planned or does not work as expected.
- You are dependent on a supplier who goes out of business.
- You implement a new web-based survey system that gets attacked by hackers.
- Your company imposes a travel freeze on non-customer-facing people.

Completion criteria

Another reason some projects fail is that their completion criteria have never been agreed. There is no way of knowing whether the work is actually complete. If your overall customer experience initiative includes a project to implement a new executive feedback process for your largest customers, some completion criteria might be:

- At least 50 customer executives interviewed.
- At least five customers covered.
- At least three customers have formally approved the resulting improvement plans.
- Customer-visible website implemented that allows customers to see progress on the improvement plan.
- Formal report-out to the business unit VP, with his or her final approval for the new process.
- Completing the interview process is in the formal goals of half the sales force, for completion within six months.

Completion criteria need to be agreed before the project starts.

Implement and experiment

Speed dating

An evocative name for an essential process. It is common that project teams identify dependencies on other teams or individuals when they write down their task plans. Surprisingly, it is also common that they never discuss the interdependencies with the people concerned. Projects then get delayed or don't succeed. Organize simple speed dating towards the end of your kickoff workshop. Each team visits each other team purely to discuss their mutual dependencies. For example, a service center may want to improve their call handling software and depend on help from IT and procurement people to make it happen. Use printed versions of each task plan to facilitate the work. You will also find some work duplication and the short speed-dating discussion should resolve it. Use a countdown timer to signal the end of each session. Ten minutes each may be enough.

Avoiding scope creep

Most major projects fail because of scope creep. By this I mean the constant addition of new deliverables; new work for the project team. It is tempting to always say 'yes' to every new request. The best way I have seen of handling this is to manage the project like a software release. You plan the pre-production Alpha version to have certain features. If someone comes along with a new request that you want to implement, you leave Alpha alone, and put the new feature into the Beta version, the final pilot. You then have production versions 1.0, 1.1 and so on. This is one of the methods to use to ensure ongoing sponsorship for your work.

The Pre-Mortem

Most project teams are excessively optimistic both about speed and success of implementation. The behavioral economist Gary Klein[23] normally believes in intuitive decision making and has made a notable suggestion. To prevent or at least limit over-optimism, he suggests a workshop with people who are knowledgeable about the decision or project, at a point where work is well advanced, but is not complete. His suggestion is to ask the team to "Imagine that we are a year into the future. We implemented the plan as it

---

[23] Gary Klein's HBR article on pre-mortems is available at https://hbr.org/2007/09/performing-a-project-premortem

now exists. The outcome was a disaster. Please take 5 to 10 minutes to write a brief history of the disaster." In my limited experience of using this technique, it is very effective indeed. The project team openly discusses concerns they had been keeping to themselves. Risks that were not in the risk monitor become evident and can be mitigated. Possible events occurring elsewhere in your company are surfaced and can be dealt with.

12.2 Types of teams you may want to implement

There are four types of teams you may want to implement to improve customer experience. This chapter covers the membership and work of each. They are:

- Customer Success teams
- Customer Advisory Boards
- Executive Sponsors
- Project Sponsors

Customer Success

Customer Success teams started in the software industry. They probably exist under various names in other industries that sell complex products. It is a concept that is useful and necessary where you have customer contracts that are renewed each year. Software companies sell a limited range of things. Licenses allow you to use software for the duration of the license, whether the application is in the Cloud or run locally. Implementation services help customers to get up and running. Technical support services are there for when things don't work as promised. Educational services provide training to users.

While that may seem complete, we often had surprises of two specific types when customers told us they no longer wanted to use our software: first, they sometimes complained that the software lacked a specific functionality that was in fact present. Second, especially with complex software, they blamed themselves if they could not get it to work as expected, and did not ask for help. Enter Customer Success teams.

Customer Success teams work with your most important customers to ensure they do indeed achieve the ROI or 'Time to Value' that they expected when they bought the software. The simplest way of thinking about it would be to consider it to be usage support. There is no charge for the service. It does not replace or duplicate any of the paid services. A Customer Success person goes to the customer site and sits with the key users, watching them use the software and suggesting how they can be more effective.

When we introduced these teams at HP, we compared support-contract renewal rates between similar types of customers that either did or did not have a Customer Success Manager assigned. (Support contracts include both the rights to use new versions of software and the ability to access technical support resources.) The effect of the Customer Success people was dramatic, bringing a spectacular improvement in renewal rates. I suppose I also need to mention that they occasionally discovered customers who had bought the software but never installed it, but had not said anything. Sales people tend not to worry too much about customers after they have been compensated for the sale, and we simply had not noticed.

Customer Success people are deep product experts. A lot of ours had worked in software R&D. Each individual tends to only be an expert in one product, two or three at best. They are therefore assigned to your top customers for that specific product, rather than your top customers overall. As distinct from the people manning support helplines, the Customer Success teams are more expert than the customer's own people. Their primary relationship is with the people using the product, rather than the ones who may have bought it. This is quite an important distinction that needs to be considered for the relationship surveys you have with your most important customers.

HP Software, like most large businesses on the planet, had about 40% of all customers in 'the deadly zone of mutual indifference'. We did not talk to them, and they did not talk to us, or at least that was the case before Customer Success teams arrived. These were the customers most likely to be susceptible to competitors showing up with attractive promises of a better life. The constant interaction with their Customer Success manager made it far less likely that these customers would switch.

If you are selling annuity contracts, it is easy to calculate the value of a one-point improvement in renewal rates. Start with your largest customers and work down. A reasonable starting principle is that one Customer Success person can handle ten customers. If, for example, you currently have an 88% contract renewal rate, calculate affordability based on a 92% renewal rate. Start with half of the relevant customer population for the first year, so you can evaluate whether it really produces the expected results. The Customer Success person should also participate in any regular meetings the sales leader for that customer may hold.

Customer Success teams discover issues that are specific to individual customers and generic things that apply to all customers. One approach to provide smaller customers some of the benefits of the investment is to record videos that show your customers how to do things that others find difficult. Make them available free of charge on your website or on YouTube.

Customer Advisory Boards

If your business has some very large customers whose success depends on your products and services, Customer Advisory Boards can be a great help. 'Very large means they spend at least $5 million annually with you. The purpose of CABs is to allow your customers to give you advice. I have seen them implemented well, and implemented poorly. The difference between the two happens when a company forgets who is supposed to be giving the advice. (Hint: the customers.)

Members should be senior executives with similar job responsibilities. The closer the members' profiles are to each other, the more they will enjoy getting together. Indeed, they are likely to continue their conversations between any meetings you may organize. I suggest having no more than about eight members. If you have more large customers, organize multiple boards, ideally by industry.

The benefit of receiving advice from key customers should be obvious, but what is the benefit to them? Here are the top three reasons the customers will want to be members:

Implement and experiment

1. The opportunity to meet their peers in other companies. Ensure you provide long, indeed very long breaks so they can interact informally. Don't let any agenda item interfere with the break times.
2. The opportunity to give you feedback about what they want you to improve. After holding an initial meeting, you should ask them to prepare such feedback in advance, presenting it at the following meeting. I suggest asking for a volunteer among the members and letting them do the work on their own.
3. The opportunity to participate in creating new products and services that address their problems and business opportunities.

Avoid treating a Customer Advisory Board as a captive audience for your marketing team. You should not be trying to sell them anything during the meetings. Ensure you treat them as an ongoing community, with regular phone, email and face-to-face interaction. Always bear in mind that they will enjoy meeting each other more than they enjoy meeting you. Ensure space for that to happen, especially as it will build a community around your products.

Executive sponsors for strategic accounts

We have discussed the concept of strategic accounts in the section about relationship surveys. A sponsor should be a senior executive who is able to devote a substantial portion of his or her time to improving the relationship your company has with an individual customer. 'Substantial' means two to four days per month. This time is almost never spent directly in selling sessions. Examples of what customer sponsors do are:

- Brief the customer's leadership team on the strategy of your company.
- Call the customer's key people to discuss your latest quarterly results. If the sponsor is, for example, your CFO, they may call the customer's CFO.
- Brief the customer on new products or services entirely outside any possible current sales opportunity.
- Brief the customer on the latest change of CEO or other senior executive.

194

Types of teams you may want to implement

- Call the customer to discuss their latest earnings announcement, product announcement or leadership changes.
- If the customer has a current escalation in progress with your company, the sponsor should call the senior executives to give them progress updates.
- Make a presentation about the customer to your company leadership team on a quarterly basis. A good practice is to have this as a regular agenda item. You can optionally invite the customer to present their company.

In essence, the executive sponsor's main role is to give the customer confidence that you are going to take care of them. Going back to the 'couples' metaphor, this is particularly important for customers who are neither very positive nor very negative about you. You should stimulate regular two-way communication.

An executive sponsor is unlikely to be successful without being personally interested in the company concerned. In my own case, an uncle founded Ireland's first cable TV company (Phoenix Relays) and I took personal interest in the cable-encryption company Kudelski, when they were an HP strategic account. I consider this to be the most important piece of screening you do. If you have nobody who is interested in a particular customer's business, I believe you will be better off not appointing anyone, rather than having someone who does not care.

Executive sponsors are also formal or informal escalation points the customer may naturally go to if they are upset about something and are not getting it resolved. Your formal escalation teams also need to keep the sponsor informed of anything serious that is going on at the customer site.

You can consider asking executive sponsors to do some of your relationship-survey interviews. They will only agree if the formal list of questions is very short, as in the NPS format. While they may be reluctant to ask the single rating question in such a survey, they will probably get over it. I suggest persuading them that it is a good way of finding out whether the person is willing to be a reference, and if not, what we need to improve to get there.

Doing the work well takes a lot of research and presence. If, for example, you have 20 strategic accounts, and have 20 or more appropriate leaders, they should take one customer each, and plan on spending five to ten hours a week on the sponsorship role, at least for the first months.

Project sponsors

The project sponsor role is defined in a White Paper by the Project Management Institute as:

- Providing clear direction for the project and how it links with the organization's overall strategy.
- Securing project resources.
- Ensuring the project is on time, on budget and on scope.
- Providing feedback on status reports and making sure they reach the necessary stakeholders.
- Championing the project at the executive level to secure buy-in.

Both customer and internal projects should have sponsors. They have as much impact as the project manager. In the case of customer projects, you can consider asking the sponsor to formally interview customer executives about the project once it is complete, or has hit major milestones.

13. Special section

Customer references

13.1 Creating and using customer references

So you have customers who are happy with your products. Some may even have told you they would like to recommend them to others. Here are the main categories of customer references and suggestions about using them, and avoiding over-use.

Telephone references

Ask an enthusiastic customer to take three phone calls from potential new customers within a month. Don't give in to the temptation to make these into conference calls. You are perfectly safe letting the existing and potential new customer have the discussion on their own. Don't put the customer in the embarrassing situation of talking to a competitor. The existing enthusiastic customer is never going to tell the new customer that he / she wasted their company's money buying your product or service. That would make them seem foolish and is counter to human nature. If you have a Customer Success team, they are ideal for managing the number of calls, and can be the custodians of the phone numbers. You may decide on a different custodian, and it is critical to ensure the reference customer does not receive more calls than they have agreed to.

These and all other types of references have a "shelf life". The commitment to be a reference should be considered to be short-term. Customers generally like being considered as experts by others. If you and your customers are happy to continue after the initial period, that should be agreed formally.

Press releases and other short-term marketing material

Marketing departments love references. As distinct from the telephone references covered above, there is almost no benefit to the customer in participating. They have no real control over who gets the messages. You may want to negotiate references as part of a sales deal. Remember that a customer may change his / her mind about your product after a few months. Agreements to use print and web references should be for a defined short period of time. If the customer's marketing department is the entity that must agree to the reference, they will expect you to propose the customer quote.

'Lighthouse' references

If you are fortunate enough to have secured your ideal, perfect customer who is *the* name in your target industry, and they love your product, you will probably be in marketing heaven. These are the customers you will invite to be on stage at your external events, and to talk to your employees. However, they are usually fully aware of the situation and will want something in return. Sometimes this is free product or at least huge discounts. Sometimes it is the ability to provide input about product direction. Your marketing department should control these references. You can decide whether or not any unusually high rebates should be part of the marketing budget.

Negative references

Whether revealed by your product surveys or by scanning the web, you probably have negative references too. Talk to them and do your best to turn them around. Don't let them fester. Don't talk to them using public forums where they may feel obliged to further defend their negative positions. Remember to apologize.

14.   Suggested schedule

14.1 Suggested timing

The timing below should work well for the largest companies. In smaller companies, you may be able to compress it a little. The workload will not be identical for all who are involved in situation analysis. The nature of customer experience strategy means that the customer, partner and competitor workstreams normally have more work to do than the others. However, if your company has grown through acquisitions, the internal-realities work will be complex. Investment approvals happen at the end of the third stage below.

Exhibit 14.1

Suggested implementation timing

Situation analysis 4-6 weeks	Strategic choices 2-3 weeks	Investments/Impact 2-3 weeks	Implementation plan 2-3 weeks
• Project lead assembles core team • Workstream leads create their teams • 6 workstreams completed • Insights presented to leadership	• Summarize situation analysis • Prepare strategic choices workshop by circulating material to other workstreams • Workshop: Each leader prepares and proposes initiatives to all other teams	• Prioritize initiatives by financial ROI and customer impact • Prepare leadership team proposal with high, medium and low investment cases	• Assemble project team for each approved initiative • Hold initial workshop to define task plan, completion criteria, risk plan • "Speed dating" to interlock workstreams

Timing considerations

The larger your company, the more likely it is that some fixed events may drive your precise program timing. Here are some things you may like to bear in mind:

- The strategy exercise should take place outside your annual planning cycle. However, they may need to be compatible. If you need to set up a substantial new incubator team for one of your initiatives, that may need to be part of your annual budgeting exercise. You therefore have less control over the timing for such

Suggested schedule

teams, and need to bear that in mind when creating the implementation plan.

- Creating the implementation plan is not the same as implementing it. This timing is about the creation only.
- Completion of each phase may require presentation to, and approval by your leadership team. They may have their meetings on a fixed schedule that you have to respect. If you are told there is no space on the agenda for your presentation, you have a different problem.
- In the northern hemisphere, budgeting cycles often start just after the summer vacation period. If your strategy cycle has to be completed just before the budget cycle starts, some of your team may not be available at critical moments.
- It is human nature that people tend to complete the tasks in the project plan just before the review call or meeting. If you believe you are falling behind your ideal timing, hold two reviews a week instead of one.

15. Conclusion

What customers want

15.1 What customers want

While I have been pushing a scientific approach to building and implementing a customer experience strategy, let's put that aside for a moment. After working in this area since 1981, there are a few things I believe are high priorities for most B2B customers. You probably won't discover some of these points directly in any formal feedback system, though they may be at the heart of many different improvement suggestions.

Remember me

Customers all want to be remembered. This means remembering everyone with whom you have had contact, and what that contact was about. Think about your favorite local restaurant. You appreciate it if the owner greets you at the door and says, "Welcome back Mrs. Smith. It is good to see you here again." It gets better if the waiter asks, "Would you like the same drink as last time?" You feel that you matter to them.

At its most trivial this means not asking customers for the same information repeatedly if they phone you for support. If your phone routing system asks them for a contract number to route them correctly, you should not ask them for the contract number again. If you have gone through a diagnosis process with a generalist and found that you need to pass it to a more specialized person, the diagnosis information should go with the call. If the person has already phoned with the same problem, or indeed any problem, you should know about it and potentially check that all is still OK. If you have the person's phone number in your database and the person calls from that number, you should not need to ask their name.

You must participate in the customer's investment process

Your company probably has a standard format for proposing solutions to customers. If your customer is a large company, they are certain to have their own investment approval process. The person you are selling to has to decide, then propose any substantial investment for further approval at their end. Your proposal needs to fit their process. You should find out what their process is, and make it as easy as possible for them to use it to get your proposal approved.

Continuity of project management

If yours is a service business that relies on project execution, ensure the same project manager is in charge from the start to the end of the engagement. Let's suppose you have three project stages: proof of concept, pilot, and full roll-out. Different people are needed for each stage of the project. If you have a completely different team for each stage, each new team leader has to get to know the customer organization, and the customer has to get to know them. Customers find full team changes deeply frustrating. The best solution for this is to keep the same project manager in charge the whole way through.

Reduction of your organizational complexity

If you are a large company, you are a complex company. Large customers are complex too, so they will have some empathy for you. A fundamental role of your account team is to reduce the perception and consequences of that complexity for customers. The account manager should be the broker between your different businesses and functions. If you have multiple businesses, each with a separate sales team, you will fail in this complexity reduction and never become a true strategic partner. You will be condemned to have their procurement department as your main contact point. This is not good for your margins.

Your company is always "We"

No matter what your customers complain about, apologize on behalf of your company. The worst type of thing you can say is "Ah yes, another complaint about shipping. Those people have a lot of problems at the moment." Replace the thinking by "I am sorry you had this experience. We have had a few shipping problems recently and are doing our best to improve."

What resellers want

If you use resellers to sell complex products, the resellers' top priority will probably be that you supply accurate, price-competitive quotations quickly. Let's suppose the reseller is selling to Nestlé, and that you have a global discount agreement directly with Nestlé that gives them a price reduction everywhere in the world. The quotation you give the reseller needs to reflect that. Let's further suppose that this deal is in Indonesia and that you have had to give a further 15% price reduction to Nestlé in Indonesia the last three times you did business there. You should give the reseller the quotation with the additional reduction without being asked, though with the necessary explanation. Otherwise you, the reseller and Nestlé all waste time.

The second thing resellers want is for you not to compete with them. Unless you have a formal business model that says you work 100% through resellers, their expectation is not realistic. Your most important customers will want to do business directly with you. The best you can do for resellers is to provide them with clarity on your business model, letting them know when they can expect you to show up, and when it is less likely. If you do business in many countries, it is also probable that you have countries where you have no direct presence and will use resellers. Sometimes you will have an exclusive agreement for a country with a single reseller. Be clear about that too.

Remember that cost reduction is not strategic

While your selling proposition to customers may be cost reduction, cost reduction is not strategic for customers. While that might not seem to make sense, try to think about it this way: the strategic decision is what to do with the money that has been saved. How will it be invested? Once you are helping customers with their investments, you access people that are higher up in the organization and develop a true strategic partnership.

Customers get used to positive experience, then expect more

With relatives in Chicago and California, the difference in weather between the two is common subject of discussion. In addition, the Californian relatives have moved there recently. I have observed this phenomenon with others who have moved to much better climates. Personally, I moved from wet and gray Galway, in the west of Ireland a long time ago, and learned to appreciate the existence of summer. However, for me, and for others who have gone through the weather-improvement experience, its impact is strongest at the start, and fades over the years. Nicer weather becomes "the new normal". So it is with customer experience. No matter how great the improvements you implement, customers will get used to them. Your competitors may also copy them. You need to repeat the whole strategy development exercise and come up with your "next big thing".

15.2 Managing change

Leading a change in any aspect of business strategy can be challenging. Changing your customer experience strategy takes time. I want to conclude this book with some practical advice on change management in this context.

The change equation

In my Digital Equipment days, senior leaders Don Gordon and Peter Mercury popularized what they called the change equation. It is fairly simple. You need three things to drive change:

1. A clear vision of a highly desirable future state.
2. Practical first steps on the path towards the vision.
3. Evidence that that it will be worth the cost and effort.

The strategy-development framework, sponsorship, and communication advice presented in earlier chapters all support the change equation. Don and Peter also had a great communication insight: the people who obviously benefit from the change you are proposing will support it, and actually don't need any particular focus. You need to work out who is likely to believe that they will lose out from the change. Concentrate your communication efforts on them.

Swiss mountain guides

Finally, I would like to leave you with one of the few Swiss management metaphors. The country is covered in mountains. Hiking up a mountain with a guide is quite common. Leading a group up a steep slope can be challenging, especially when the group members have differing levels of fitness. The guide must encourage and support their progress. Inexperienced guides believe that if they go further and further ahead of the group, the group will speed up. They will not. At best, the group will stop moving. At worst, they will go back down the mountain without you. A great guide leads from within the group.

Conclusion

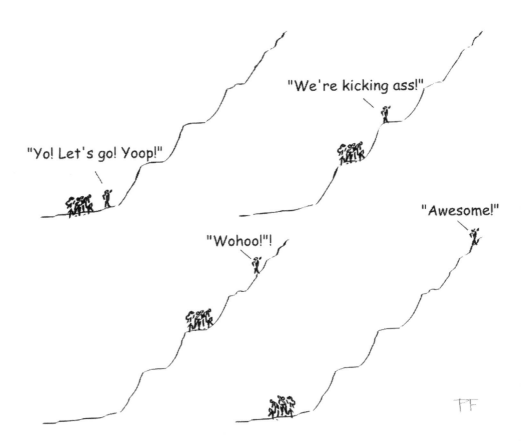

Appendix 1

Situation Analysis questions

Here is a more complete list of questions than the one provided earlier in this book.

Customers

This team asks and answers questions about what customer experience expectations your customers have had up to now and how you expect them to change in the future. Here are some sample questions that may help get you started:

- What experiences do your traditional end-customers want at the most important customer journey points? How reliable is your evidence for this?
- How and why are the expectations of your traditional customers changing over time?
- Are there useful ways you could segment customers and provide differentiated experiences to each segment? Should all customers of all sizes and from all industries be treated exactly the same or should you tailor a specific experience for each?
- Should new customers be treated differently from existing customers? If so, how?
- If you provide both face-to-face and web-based purchase and post-sales experiences, is the intent that one should complement and build on the other, or are they set up to effectively compete for customer attention? If they compete with each other, is that your intention, or just the result of the way you have set up the work of two independent teams? Are the prices the same, no matter what the purchase channel?
- Do you have any information on how your traditional customers consider their experiences with you compared to what they experience with competitors?
- What do your formal feedback mechanisms tell you about customer experience expectations?

Situation analysis questions

- Do you currently communicate back to customers, telling them what you are doing with input they have provided?
- Which are the areas where you just have to be 'good enough' and investing more does not provide much return?
- Are new types of customers emerging with different expectations?
- What experiences are you providing customers that give you no competitive advantage and could be stopped to provide resources for new work?
- Do some of your customers have supplier assessment processes in place? If so, how are you doing in their ratings?
- If customers have left you, or you unexpectedly lost a deal you expected to win, do you understand why?
- If you have an executive sponsor program and / or a Customer Advisory Board in place for your largest customers, do you have any way of getting consensus from the sponsors and the board on the most important improvement opportunities?

At least half the day-to-day work of most customer experience teams is about listening to customers and partners, then summarizing what they want you to improve. This means that much of the necessary situation analysis information is directly expected from, and controlled by the customer experience leader. Naturally, in small companies, there is no single central reference point, except perhaps the owner or CEO.

Partners

The majority of companies have partners for at least some of their business. The three main categories of partners available to most businesses are resellers, implementation partners, and subcontractors. While you may have some partners who do not work with anyone else, it is more likely that you compete for their attention. Here are some possible questions that may help you to get started with the partner analysis:

- What are the critical touchpoints for your resellers, implementation partners and subcontractors? How have these been changing over time? Are these three categories useful, or is there a better way to segment your partners from a partner experience perspective?

- Should the top few partners, in terms of revenue generation, be treated differently from the rest?
- How does your partners' experience with your company compare to that with your traditional and emerging competitors?
- Who are your potential new partners, and why?
- Which partnerships are not producing anything useful and should be fixed or stopped?
- How do your partner marketing incentives compare to those of your competitors?
- How do your partner payment terms compare to those offered by your competitors?
- How quickly are resellers able to access any special pricing agreements you may have in place for very large customers?
- Do you compete directly with your partners?
- If you have a formal partner survey mechanism, what has it taught you?

Competitors

There are two main categories of competitors: traditional and emerging. The emerging category includes companies you do not know about yet, but who may be about to take over your market. There are industries such as steel manufacturing where barriers to entry are high, and you are unlikely to be surprised. There are also low-barrier industries such as software, and pure import-export businesses. Here are some questions that may help analyze the competition:

- Do you have competitive benchmark survey data that lets you understand where your competitors provide a superior experience and the situations or touchpoints where you lead. If so, how do you compare with traditional competitors and are new competitors emerging with differentiated customer experience?
- How have competitors' customer experience strategy and results changed over time? What investments have they been making in people and systems? (Going to their website to look at their list of job openings may help with this.)

Situation analysis questions

- What do your critical competitors say about customer focus and customer experience in their quarterly and annual reports? Is customer experience mentioned on their website as a formal part of their business strategy? How have they set up their customer experience teams and others that support critical touchpoints?
- What customer experience software and consulting companies use your competitors as references on their websites?
- Do you have competitors that have no short-term profit objective and so can outspend you in critical customer experience areas?
- If another company is the customer experience star in your industry, what are the two or three most important reasons for the leadership? Are you able to do those two or three things better than the competitor, or should you be concentrating on doing things differently? (Both work.)
- What customer-experience-related investments have your competitors stopped or radically decreased?
- Do you see competitors whose customer experience approach differs by country?

Customer experience industry trends

All industries change over time. Customer experience itself has been changing, from at least two perspectives. First, the products and service offerings that help companies to provide better customer and partner experience change over time. Second, there are industry-specific customer-experience changes. For example, 'Customer Success Teams' have been implemented by most large software vendors over the last five years or so. These teams help customers to install and understand software, free of charge. Here are some questions that should help this part of the analysis:

- What is happening in the customer experience industry? What ways of listening to customers are most popular? What new improvement processes and technologies are emerging?
- What is the impact of social media on customer perception of your products and services? Do you know what is being said about you on social media, and does it matter?
- Which measurement systems best predict revenue and market share?

- How do the latest developments compare with what you are currently using?
- What customer experience competitive benchmark data is available and relevant to your industry?

External environment

These questions are about the environment in which your company, your competitors and your customers live. It includes government regulation and general concerns and hopes of the people in countries where you operate. You may find these questions useful:

- How does government regulation affect the way you want to go about measuring and improving customer experience?
- What current and emerging rules about data privacy affect your current and potential survey processes?
- How are you required to maintain customer survey opt-out lists?
- Do you know what surveys are being run in your company and whether they respect relevant laws?
- Are you allowed to transmit customer lists to subcontractors such as survey providers?
- Do some governments and countries where you operate have an unusually high focus on the environment, gender equality, fighting corruption or other formal initiatives that you may find useful in building your brand image?

Internal realities

While the first five areas are all about what is happening outside your company, you are unlikely to be able to sell and implement every conceivable idea within your company. These questions may help establish what you can achieve:

- What is the state of executive sponsorship for your current efforts?
- How likely are you to be to get any additional funding and people you may need to implement?
- What can you do to prove the value of your work?

Situation analysis questions

- How can you secure enduring sponsorship for your work; sponsorship that will survive leadership changes?
- What current work can you stop in your own area to provide resources for new work?
- Do you have a formal talent management program in your company that you could use to staff improvement work on a part-time basis?
- What measurement and improvement systems and processes have your CEO and other key leaders used in their previous companies?
- Look at the intranet pages of your business and function leaders. Which ones mention customers as a priority and which seem to have no interest in the topic? Which ones have announced and staffed formal customer-centric initiatives?
- Have you grown by mergers and acquisitions? If so, are many different improvement systems and processes in place? Which ones seem to have the best reputations and produce superior results?

Index